Teaching from the Heart and Soul

D0067651

TEACHING FROM THE HEART AND SOUL

The Robert F. Panara Story

Harry G. Lang

Gallaudet University Press
Washington, D.C.

Gallaudet University Press
Washington, D.C. 20002
http://gupress.gallaudet.edu

Cover photograph: Courtesy of the Gallaudet University Archives

Library of Congress Cataloging-in-Publication Data
Lang, Harry G.
    Teaching from the heart and soul : the Robert F. Panara story / Harry G. Lang.
        p. cm.
    Includes bibliographical references and index.
    ISBN-13: 978-1-56368-358-9 (alk. paper)
    1. Panara, Robert.   2. Deaf—United States—Biography.   3. Teachers of
the deaf—United States—Biography.   4. Deaf authors—United States—
Biography.   5. Poets, American—20th century—Biography.   6. Acting
teachers—United States—Biography.   I. Title.
    HV2534.P36L36   2007
    371.91′2—dc22
    [B]

                                                                2007006552

This book is dedicated to the memory and spirit of Shirley Panara, who showed that there is no end to the power of a beloved wife, mother, and friend in affecting our journeys through life.

Contents

Foreword

This adventure in narrating the life of Robert F. Panara began one evening in late August 2002. My wife, Bonnie Meath-Lang, a professor of performing arts and literature, and I joined Bob and his wife, Shirley, at a baseball game to watch the Rochester (New York) Red Wings, the city's Triple A farm team. We were about a week away from the start of the school year, and this was our last chance to see a game as a foursome that season. Soon Bonnie would be tied up with theater rehearsals in the evenings. Shirley had been fighting a long battle with cancer, but she remained in good spirits. Although the leukemia had gone into remission, she often tired by 9:00 pm. When she was able to join Bob and me at a game, she would usually drive her own car to the stadium so that she could leave a little earlier. She nevertheless made the most of the earlier hours of the evening with her consistently positive attitude.

On this evening, we were chatting between innings when Bob left his seat to get some hot pretzels. Shirley waited until he was out of sight, then turned to me and privately asked me, "Would you consider writing a biography of Bob?"

I was stunned for a moment. I felt honored that she would invite me to write his life story, but she had also caught me by surprise. More than thirty years' worth of memories began to flood my thoughts. I thought back to the 1974–1975 school year at the National Technical Institute for the Deaf (NTID) at Rochester Institute of Technology (RIT). That spring, Bob was honored with the prestigious Eisenhart Award for Outstanding Teaching. This, in my opinion, was one of his greatest moments. I have known Bob for thirty-seven years and have frequently observed how much he is revered by his students and virtually everyone who knows him. I quickly realized the importance of Shirley's request: If a narration of Bob's personal journey into teaching could help a new generation of teachers see how his excellence in the classroom can be achieved through a lifelong pursuit of beliefs, values, knowledge, and skills, then the effort to document his life would be well worth the time.

Bob is a poet, book author, lecturer, and theater aficionado. As a young deaf boy, he was largely self-educated in the mainstream (in public schools) in an era when special accommodations were not yet available for deaf children. He was also among the first wave of deaf scholars in the twentieth century, and a pioneer in the field of Deaf Studies. Bob's experiences were distinctive, but his life was also a microcosm of the "Deaf experience"—one man's response to the many debates that have surrounded the education of deaf students.

Bob is also a baseball buff, and after Shirley's invitation it occurred to me that I could write an entire book about his life as a baseball fan. Indeed, for years I had been begging Bob to write his own baseball stories, much as the writer Stephen King had long encouraged Stephen Jay Gould to write his book *Triumph and Tragedy in Mudville: A Lifelong Passion for Baseball.* Bob's baseball memoirs would have been unique and funny.

Although baseball is one of the threads that has held Bob's life together—and made it colorful—if I focused on Bob's teaching, I would be able to capture only a few of the baseball stories.

On the other hand, teaching is Bob's real legacy. At Gallaudet College, his respected mentor Powrie Vaux Doctor had told him, "I believe your niche in life is to be a teacher of the deaf."[1] Through the years that I worked with Bob at NTID I often saw him inspiring his own students to, in his own words, "do something with their life that will be rewarding and satisfying."[2]

In the short time Bob had been gone from his seat at the baseball stadium, I gladly accepted Shirley's invitation to tell the story of Bob's life. The details would be worked out later. When Bob returned with the hot pretzels and Shirley shared with him the gist of our discussion, he grinned with surprise and stuck out his hand in appreciation. That hand had once been grasped by such baseball greats as Babe Ruth, Joe DiMaggio, and Brooks Robinson, I thought.

It was time to get back to watching the game!

Over the next few months, I pored through boxes of newspaper clippings, letters, magazine articles, videotapes, old high school and college yearbooks, and Bob's teaching materials. Though Bob was generally conceded upon his retirement in 1987 to be one of the best teachers in the field of educating deaf students, I did not know where to begin. Bob had often spoken about how several of his former teachers had inspired him, most notably Lloyd Harrison at the American School for the Deaf, Frederick Hughes at Gallaudet College, and, of course, the legendary Powrie Vaux Doctor, known affectionately as

"Doc," but what was it about Bob's teaching that had led him to touch the lives of an enormous number of people? One evening I found an obscure article that grabbed my attention. It was a term paper for one of his courses at Gallaudet, and Doc had liked it so much that he encouraged Bob to publish it. Bob had written "The Significance of the Reading Problem" when he was still an undergraduate college student.

"What the world needs today," Bob wrote in 1944, "is more teaching that comes from the heart and soul, and not of the coldly conservative and somewhat reticent mind."[3]

For me, that precocious pronouncement defined Bob's own teaching. He had defined his teaching ideal before he ever taught his first class. When he wrote this essay, he was still in his early twenties and remarkably well read. Now, six decades later, I set out to examine how this man had achieved this ideal so effectively that generations of his former students fondly remembered his classes and remained his friends well into his retirement years. That evening, in early October 2002, I set out to answer the research question to be addressed in this biography: What had Bob meant by "teaching that comes from the heart and soul"?

Although this book was written for the "Deaf Lives" series for Gallaudet University Press, I believe it can be read and enjoyed by anyone who has a passion for teaching (or for baseball). The issues surrounding deafness and sign language were part of Bob's life, but the characteristics of a master teacher that Bob developed were those that would make any teacher exemplary, regardless of that person's own hearing status or that of his students. One challenge for me was to summarize Bob's life in a way that could be appreciated by a broad audience, not just those in Deaf education.

A second challenge was related to the "Deaf Lives" series. Each book in this series includes some relevant scholarly analysis, and my task involved writing a biography of a living person. Many distinguished writers have described the difficulties in staying free of the shadow cast by a respected subject. Some have advised that keeping a certain distance is essential to a successful biography, emphasizing the importance of remaining in charge of one's own work. The author, most seem to agree, needs to freely interpret the information available.

In his review of Richard Schickel's life story of the stage and screen director Elia Kazan, John Simon wrote in the *New York Times* that "a good biography is like a good marriage." The biographer and his subject must have a "discriminatingly nuanced rather than blind" attachment, especially if they know each other personally.[4] When Bob began calling me his "Boswell," referring to Samuel Johnson's friend and biographer, I felt this was a great compliment, although the only thing I may have in common with Boswell is that I am about three decades younger than my subject. Subconsciously, I did practice some of Boswell's conventions, however. I took notes of Bob's conversations for several years and became absorbed with his interactions with others. The proverbial deaf man's pad and pencil had become for me, especially at baseball and hockey games, a note-taking system during the many conversations we had.

I also inject myself, initially in this Foreword, and later in the book, occasionally embellishing the biography with conversations between Bob and myself. Probably the most important parallel with Boswell's *Life of Johnson* and my biography of Bob Panara, however, is how Bob's life story illustrates a point—in this case how one great teacher was shaped by his life experiences and by the powerful influence of other great teachers.

John Simon also writes that one challenge that all biographers experience is how to be tactful—deciding what should go into the biography and what to leave out. At times I knew that Bob would have wanted to include certain anecdotes. He sometimes seemed intent on reminiscing about things that his college chums would enjoy reading about. There were other stories that he cherished, but I could not fit them in comfortably. I had to decide which aspects of Bob's life were most important to me as the biographer and how I wanted to portray them in relation to his teaching, keeping in mind the audience of readers who, I hope, will enjoy and learn from this book. Admittedly, there are more dimensions to Bob's life than are possible to deal with in one biography. More than a few of you who know Bob may have bought this book out of curiosity about how I bring together poetry, baseball, and teaching. I found that these aspects of Bob's life have been so interwoven that it would be difficult to tell his story any other way.

In developing a methodological approach for the research for this book, I studied what other biographers, and their reviewers, had to say about writing about a living person. "In order to be able to write a biography," says Patrick French, you have to "understand the cultural background of your subject."[5] I felt comfortable in this regard. Bob and I had both become profoundly deaf in early adolescence from spinal meningitis. While writing this biography, I have more than a few times relived my own experiences in adjusting to profound deafness as a young boy. On one hand, the experiences we had in common gave me powerful insight. I had experienced firsthand many things that Bob went through in his adjusting to deafness. Like Bob, I was left much to my own devices as a child searching for meaning and direction in life. On the other hand, I had to resist the temptation to interject my own experiences. Working closely with Bob, through hundreds of chats and thousands of e-mail notes, and through privileged access to his unpublished private writings, I came to believe that the value of distance and detachment can be balanced with personal empathy. Such a combination would make the biography really come to life for the reader. And as I hope the reader will see in this biography, one of Bob's own goals as a teacher has always been to make books come alive.

Writing a biography of Bob Panara also meant that I would become absorbed not only with his past but also his present. Bob's wife, Shirley, and I became even better friends, and I got to know his son, John, and, through correspondence and Bob's stories, his other family members. Bob's good friends became important people in my own life, and I understood his joys and frustrations as if they were my own. In seeking how best to assemble the mosaic of Bob's life, I heeded the advice of Jay Parini, who wrote in the *Chronicle of Higher Education* that good biographers need to become "fiction-makers." "That doesn't mean that they invent facts," he explained. "Rather, they put them in a particular order, shaping them, placing an emphasis here and not there, dramatizing events that may, to the subject of the biography, have seemed undramatic at the time.

. . . They create, or discover, a story that was hiding in plain sight—even from the subject."[6] This was made a bit easier by the fact that Bob has always been a pack rat, right down to his elementary school autograph book. More important, he saved boxes of videotapes of his teaching, he kept old course notes, "videoletters" with the deaf filmmaker Ernest Marshall, and taped interviews with notable deaf persons.

For the reader who is unfamiliar with Deaf education, let me briefly explain a long-standing controversy, which surfaces here and there in Bob's journey. It is known as the communications debate, or more poignantly as the "War of Methods," and this battle has been fought for several hundred years. Those who advocate oralism usually shun the use of sign language and stress the use of speech and speechreading (lipreading). For much of the nineteenth century in the United States, most deaf children learned through sign language, but as oralism, a movement strongly advocated by Alexander Graham Bell, took hold, not only did the use of sign language decrease in the schools, but many excellent deaf teachers lost their jobs because they could not teach speech. Decades later, in the 1960s, researchers were able to demonstrate that American Sign Language (ASL) is a true language. It has its own syntax and idioms and is not just a visual representation of spoken English. At the same time, mass media, especially the film industry, theater, and television, began to portray deaf characters and signing in ways that brought increased awareness of ASL. Sign language interpreting also grew as a profession, and ASL courses in universities and other programs attracted many new people to the beauty of this visual language.

Bob Panara taught deaf students in the midst of these revolutions, yet, one thing remained unchanged throughout these years. Most teachers, whether teaching in elementary and high schools or colleges and universities, are faced with heterogeneous classes. Some students are native ASL signers, while others know no ASL, or else they sign in English word order. Teachers have always been challenged to find a way to communicate effectively to all students, regardless of their preferred form of communication. Some argue that they prefer not to speak while signing. The clarity of signing sometimes suffers as a result. The issues became very political for decades and remain so today. Meanwhile, the politics of "mainstreaming" have reversed the pattern of deaf student enrollments. Today, more than eight out of every ten deaf students are educated in integrated settings, rather than in all-deaf residential or center school programs.

Somehow, in both high school and college environments, and in both all-deaf and integrated classes, Bob Panara developed a mix of teaching strategies that worked well and endeared him to his students. They passionately remember his courses, whether they grew up as native ASL signers, were orally educated, or something in between. The evidence of this excellence is in those stacks of boxes in Bob's basement—hundreds of letters from former students who became poets and writers, and who succeeded in other fields. They expressed their appreciation for the inspiration and the high-quality education he provided. These students are part of Bob's legacy.

This biography invites the reader to explore ways of emulating Bob's ability to touch the lives of others. Whether through the signed or printed word, he invited his audiences into his world of baseball, family, literature, drama, poetry, and Deaf Studies. Bob Panara's legacy is, more than anything else, one of cultivating in others an appreciation for the power of language.

Acknowledgments

To my wife, Bonnie Meath-Lang, a thousand thanks for our many discussions while I worked on this book—from everything about theater and poetry to the passion we share with Bob Panara for teaching deaf students. To John, Janis, Erin, and Bill Panara, and Bob's sister Eleanor Lynch, your reminiscences were heartfelt. To the late Shirley Panara, I dedicate this book. Her invitation to write Bob's biography brought new meaning to the words "best friend."

I am indebted to Jill Welks, Kathleen Sullivan Smith, Susan Stevenson Coil, and Patricia Mudgett-DeCaro, whose voices are in this work through their superb critiques. I am grateful also to Linda Coppola, Jonathan Millis, Becky Simmons, Jody Sidlauskas, and Joan Naturale from the Rochester Institute of Technology's Wallace Memorial Library, and to Michael Olson, Ulf Hedberg, and Thomas Harrington from the Edward C. Merrill Learning Center at Gallaudet University, for their research assistance. Thanks also to Mark Benjamin for his excellent work with the photographs.

I am also indebted to Brenda Brueggemann and Ivey Pittle Wallace, who were quick to appreciate the importance of a biography of an outstanding deaf teacher and its potential to touch the lives of a new generation of teachers, and to the staff of Gallaudet University Press, especially Deirdre Mullervy and Jill Porco, for their thorough and excellent support in bringing the manuscript to fruition as a published book.

To Bob Panara, I paraphrase Archibald MacLeish, "A biography should not mean, but be." Telling your story has proven to be a precious experience I will cherish for the rest of my days.

Magic

On a sunny afternoon in May 1931, ten-year-old Bob Panara and a neighbor, Gene Abbati, took the elevated interborough train to Yankee Stadium from where they lived on 231st Street and White Plains Road. The El was much nicer than the trolley car, with a panoramic view from the high rails of the Upper Bronx all the way to Fordham Road. They passed the Bronx Zoo and approached the Lower Bronx with its many tenement buildings.

Bob's bout with spinal meningitis a few months earlier had left him profoundly deaf—and also left him wondering about everything. How was he going to learn in school? How could he communicate with his parents? Could a deaf man become a baseball pro? He had never heard of one.

As the train sped toward the stadium, Bob could feel the rhythmic clatter of the train wheels on the steel tracks, and he enjoyed reading the various advertisements mounted above the train windows. At 161st Street, Yankee Stadium came into view, and they had a quick glimpse of the field over the bleacher wall. Getting off at that station, Bob's excitement about seeing another game grew as he saw the crowds pouring into the stadium. It was still early in the season, and many men were dressed in shirts and ties; ladies were also there, with their wide-brimmed hats. He and Gene found their seats in the lower deck, about thirty rows behind the Yankee dugout.

Gene then motioned to Bob to follow him, and, puzzled, Bob accompanied his neighbor down to the dugout, where Gene handed something to the usher, who nodded and left.

A few minutes later, much to Bob's surprise, Babe Ruth walked out of the dugout at Yankee Stadium clutching a letter. Babe looked around and saw Bob and Gene standing near the dugout. As the Great Bambino approached them, he spoke briefly with Abbati, then turned to Bob, smiled, and asked, "How you feeling, kid?"

Babe Ruth extended his big hand, which wrapped itself around young Bob Panara's like a catcher's mitt. Then he noticed the Saint Joseph medal that Bob's mother, Maria, had pinned to the lapel of Bob's jacket. The plan had worked. She had known that the Babe was Catholic, and she hoped it might catch the baseball player's attention.

The game was about to begin, and the Babe was in a hurry. He patted Bob on the head, said, "Glad to meet you," and smiled again.

"He loomed as large as a giant to me," Bob reminisced about this childhood encounter. "And then he was gone, waving as he left, both to us and to the people in the stands. It was the kind of thrill and experience you never forget!"[1]

Babe Ruth was a player every baseball fan looked up to. He was one of Bob's first heroes. Bob swung a pretty mean bat himself and had impressed his friends with his long ball. Like every other kid, he wondered if he might someday be a baseball legend like the Babe. Bob only wished his father could be with him. All of the baseball games during the Great Depression were played in the afternoon. The day Bob met the Babe, his father could not risk taking the afternoon off. Gene Abbati played the flute at Carnegie Hall and was free most afternoons. He was excited about this opportunity to help John and his wife, Maria. After all, he would welcome the chance to meet Ruth himself.

At the time, the Panara family was living on the upper floor of a two-story home in the Bronx owned by Gene's father, Hugo Abbati. Bob's father, John Panara, was an ardent Yankees fan and equally ardent in his belief that Bob's deafness was not permanent. John hoped and prayed, with a logic that we sometimes find curious in parents, that perhaps, if Bob could meet the great Babe Ruth, he might be shocked into hearing again. The letter he had written to Yankee Stadium officials elicited a reply, and he was pleased to learn that the arrangements could be made.

Bob recalled in detail every minute of that afternoon in Yankee Stadium leading up to his meeting with Ruth. Afterwards, everything became a blur. He watched the game, but he has absolutely no recollection of who won or even of the name of the visiting team. "Mostly, I kept looking at my little hand, and saying over and over—I shook hands with Babe Ruth!"[2]

"But," he recalls, "I still remained deaf as a post."[3]

The Silent Hours Steal On

During the months after Bob became deaf—on his mother's birthday, January 19, 1931—his father tried many things to restore his son's hearing. Some attempts were painful. All proved futile. For several weeks, a doctor gave Bob injections that caused his body to become alternately too hot or too cold. He would throw off the bedcovers and then pile on the blankets as the heat and chills came. Another Manhattan specialist placed Bob in a chair with a device strapped to his head that sent electric shocks into his ear. He could do nothing except grip the arms of the chair and tough it out. Bob's father persisted in trying these and other questionable remedies. "After four or five failures with such cures," Bob recalled, "Dad came to his senses—no doubt his shrinking bank account played a role in that decision, too."[1]

Many deaf people who are over the age of fifty recall cures their own parents tried in order to help them hear again. Some were indeed extreme, including voodoo doctors and airplane dives. Even the famous aviator Charles Lindbergh would charge families fifty dollars for "Deaf Flights." But Bob Panara is likely the only deaf person in history whose father attempted to shock him into hearing with what we might call the "Bambino

Maria and John Panara with Bob at age five.

Method." All it left him with was a feeling of euphoria over
having met Babe Ruth.

Indeed, it was a difficult time financially as well. The Panaras
sought strength and reassurance from each other as the Great
Depression took its toll. A Deaf Flight was a luxury that the

family could not afford. When Bob's sister, Eleanor, was born on August 20, 1929, the little girl brought joy to the family, but within a few months, the stock market had crashed. Chaos erupted in the banking system, and many immigrants accepted what work they could find. John Panara and his brother Ed remained with the small garment business they had started. Like other immigrants, some of the Panara family's Italian friends returned to Europe, giving up on the American dream.

Bob Panara's adventurous spirit can be traced back to his grandfather, Federico Panara, who was born in Sulmona, Abruzzi, Italy, a region known for its many beautiful churches dating back to Roman times. As a young man, Federico was a fierce patriot. In the early 1860s, he left the University of Rome, where he was studying medicine, to join the Red Shirts of Giuseppe Garibaldi, the army formed to liberate Italy from Austria. Seriously wounded by cannon shrapnel during a battle, he was hospitalized with an infected leg, which doctors decided to amputate. When Federico heard this, he took a pistol from under his pillow and threatened to shoot anyone who tried to amputate his leg. He ordered them to call his brother, Marco, who was the country's assistant surgeon general.

Marco Panara saved his brother's leg, but Federico was left with a permanent limp. Feeling that he would not qualify for medical school, the impetuous young man became disillusioned and turned to drink and gambling. After returning to Abruzzi, Federico took various clerical jobs related to medicine and the library. He married Concetta D'Ottavio, and they had five children. Bob Panara's father, Giovanni (John) Panara, was born in 1889 in Castelvecchio, a province of Aquila, Abruzzi.

Federico looked to America for a new lease on life. He and his family arrived in New York City in 1901 and settled on

Mulberry Street in the region now known as Little Italy. There Federico, who had previously learned some English in Italy, not only straightened out his own life, but was able to offer advice and translation services to other Italian immigrants arriving in New York.

Bob's father, John, only twelve years old at the time the Panaras arrived in New York, took part-time jobs to support his family. Through the next few years, he attended night school while working in the garment industry. He also became proficient in English and earned his naturalization papers in 1917 to become an American citizen. After that, he followed in his father's footsteps and helped many Italian immigrants to study and pass the naturalization examinations.

Bob's mother, Maria Perrotta, was a young woman whose family had also emigrated from Italy to America a little after the turn of the century. She attended school in New York, finished eighth grade, and began working at the age of sixteen, where she met John Panara on the same job shift. John and Maria married in 1917. While living in a fifth-floor Bronx apartment house with John's parents, his brother, Ed, and a sister, Pierina, who was infirm, Maria gave birth to a child, who died from the Spanish influenza at the age of eight months.

Three years later, on July 8, 1920, John and Maria welcomed with great joy the birth of a healthy son, Roberto Frederic Panara. Bob's middle name honors his grandfather.

In 1925, when Bob was five, his family moved to the Upper Bronx. By then, his grandmother and aunt had both died, and Federico and Ed remained with Bob and his parents. There Bob attended P.S. 103, better known as the Bronx Parkway

Public School. He was a precocious and fun-loving child and, by the age of ten, had skipped a half grade in school.

Music had always been an important part of the Panara family. Bob's father, John, had taught himself how to play both the guitar and the piano. He also loved the Metropolitan Opera. John's brother, Ed, five years younger, was more attuned to the contemporary jazz of the era and often went down to Manhattan on Saturday nights to go dancing at the clubs. He knew some of the regulars, including the comedian George Burns and the actor George Raft.

Bob's grandfather was also a music lover. Federico's younger brother, Carlo Panara, had become a well-known harpist in Europe. The Panara family's interest in music was also shared with close friends, including Dr. Ettore Tresca, who had also emigrated from Abruzzi, Italy, and built a successful practice in New York's Park Avenue district. Tresca was the personal physician of the great operatic tenor Enrico Caruso. Federico Panara also knew Caruso and owned several of the legendary tenor's charcoal caricatures, for which he was also well known.

John and Federico frequently charmed Bob with romantic tales of the family's Italian heritage and cultivated in him a thirst for knowledge. Bob sang songs in Italian with his dad, among them "Ave Maria," "Santa Lucia," and "Funiculi, Funicula."

Federico, who always wore clean white shirts, was one of Bob's favorite storytellers. His grandfather could speak four languages. When Federico died in 1929 after a hard-fought battle with cancer, the house seemed much more silent.

Then on January 19, 1931, the pleasures of music in the Panara family came to an abrupt halt. Bob's temperature soared. The ten-year-old had contracted spinal meningitis and fallen into a coma. Maria was stricken with fear. Memories of the loss of her first child haunted her. She was nursing Eleanor, and she begged John to call his friend Dr. Tresca. The good doctor came to see Bob immediately and without hesitation rushed him to the hospital.

After being in a coma for ten days, Bob regained consciousness in the hospital room. All he saw were white walls. His vision was blurred, and his eyes were crossed from his weakened condition. Everything appeared double—windows, beds, nurses. He had no feeling in his right arm. His first encounter with a nurse was strangely silent. He soon came to the shocking realization that he was profoundly deaf.

Over the next several weeks, Bob's health improved. His eyes straightened, and he regained mobility in his arm. But like many children who become deaf through spinal meningitis, he quickly learned that he had a serious vertigo problem. He could hardly take a few steps without losing his balance. The subsequent months of recovery were discouraging. Many a day went by when Bob wondered whether he would ever be able to play baseball on the sandlot again. He thought about his deafness and worried about whether his friends would have the patience to try to communicate with him. The simplest things were now a struggle, and the thought of being deaf for the rest of his life paralyzed him with fear.

It was Dr. Tresca who presented the Panara family with the chilling news that not only was Bob totally deaf, he would remain so. Bob's auditory nerves had been permanently damaged by the high fever he had experienced while in the coma. There was nothing that could be done. The doctor would be invaluable in helping Maria and John with the adjustments still ahead. Ettore Tresca had saved Bob's life, and for this the family was grateful.

Nevertheless, it was not easy for Bob's parents to accept his deafness. John became distraught, sold the family piano, and never again played his beloved guitar. Maria, after experiencing the loss of one child and a difficult birth with Bob, was relieved that Bob had survived the bout with meningitis, but she wasn't sure how to handle a deaf son.

"Learn to adapt, cope with it, and let life go on," Dr. Tresca advised them. As so many other families have had to do out of necessity, Bob's parents adjusted slowly, letting him return to everyday life at his own pace. This was no easy task. Yet, when Bob looked back, he felt that the best thing his parents did for him at this time in his life was to not overprotect him.

Bob's silent hours were filled with anxiety. Would his friends still accept him now that he was deaf? Should he return to P.S. 103? Would he ever hear again? What would a life as a deaf person be like? These and many other questions at times overwhelmed him, and he would retreat to his small bedroom to be alone with his thoughts.

As the months went by, he spent much of his time in bed reading books that his cousins brought to him from the library. He immersed himself in children's classics—*Tarzan, Treasure Island, The Three Musketeers,* and the Tom Swift series. With his love for sports, he devoured the Frank Merriwell at Yale series, about a true-blue, all-American boy who excelled in every sport and also in character, good manners, and good deeds.

Although such reading filled Bob's need, he very much missed playing sports himself. In March and April, several months after his hospitalization, he renewed his friendships with his buddies. It was springtime, and baseball season had arrived. The neighborhood had many lots, and he knew how to catch, throw, and bat. So he looked forward to the time when the weather would be nice enough to allow him and his friends to be on the field again.

There was no organized Little League at this time. Bob and his friends created their own teams, using the nicknames for the various neighborhood groups like the Wakefields, the Laconias, the Gun Hill Roaders, and the "Yonkers." Each was followed by a major league baseball team name such as the Giants or Dodgers. Bob's team was the Wakefield Yankees.

For many weeks after his meeting with Babe Ruth, Bob bragged in the sandlots about his good fortune. "I did grow a couple of sizes bigger in the eyes of my playmates."

But Bob soon learned that baseball would be a new game for him—not just a *silent* one, but also a game that would require many adjustments. The first lesson to be learned about his deafness came as a shock. A fly ball was hit to his position at center field—and he could not catch it! He tried again and again, each time either misjudging the ball badly or, worse, losing his balance and falling down awkwardly in a dizzying spiral.

Kids being kids, his friends at first broke out in laughter, but they soon realized Bob's plight. After struggling through a few games, Bob was able to regain most of his skill in fielding and rifling the ball accurately. High fly balls remained a problem. He quickly became [in his words] a "catcher in the sly," accommodating the vertigo problem by playing shortstop and letting the pitcher or infielders catch any pop-ups in his area. As he had before his bout with meningitis, he continued to impress his buddies with his hitting power, which more than compensated for the balance problem that made it difficult to catch fly balls.

Bob's vertigo problem was much more serious while swimming. A few months after Bob's recovery, the Panara family went on an outing to Orchard Beach, east of the Bronx on Pelham Bay. Bob's father was an excellent swimmer and had taught Bob to swim when he was about seven years old. Arriving at the beach in his swimsuit, Bob immediately ran to the water, waded in, walked out to shoulder-high depth, and then began to swim to the float about fifty feet out in the water. No problem— and his father naturally kept pace with him.

Climbing aboard the float, Bob ran to the diving board, sprang up, and dived into the ocean. He had done this many times before and was not expecting what would happen next: Bob completely lost his orientation underwater. Everything was sea green, and he was swallowing water as he floundered around. He could not find the surface. Bob was fortunate to have his father nearby. John pulled him onto the float.

Realizing that Bob was experiencing the balance problem from his bout with meningitis, John told Bob to dive off the board again. Bob was surprised at his father's insistence. He dove off the float again—with the same results. After fishing him out a second time, John told him to try a third time, but this time he advised Bob to keep his eyes wide open, hold his breath, and stay calm. If he would simply let his body straighten out and float upward to the surface, he would be fine.

Thanks to his father's persistence, Bob quickly learned the secret of saltwater buoyancy. Through practice, he developed strategies on his own, like blowing small bubbles from his lips and following their upward ascent to the surface. He became a good swimmer, especially over long distances, with a smooth, natural stroke. Once again, Bob demonstrated his ability to accommodate with a can-do attitude.

From Bob's home near White Plains Road the walk to the best skating pond on Van Cortlandt Park was a good three miles. No matter how cold and windy the weather, Bob and his friends would take the walk just to ice-skate on the big frozen pond. There they also played impromptu hockey games three on three—sometimes perilously close to falling through thin ice when they went sliding past the warning signs while chasing a wayward puck that missed the "net" made from a broken tree limb. This interest in hockey led Bob to join the Police Athletic League, which sponsored hockey games—not on ice, but on roller skates and in the street. The police, striving to keep kids from roller-skating where there was dangerous traffic, would close down a street outside a city or neighborhood school on Saturday mornings for these games. Sports, especially baseball, swimming, and hockey, were the girders and trusses of the bridge that Bob built to link his former childhood in the hearing world to his new world of silence. Their visual nature offered a respite from the daily challenges of communication. At this point in his life, his love for sports was all that he needed to keep old friendships and build a few new ones.

During his elementary school years Bob had especially enjoyed trips to the local movie theater to see silent movies. Perhaps it was prescient that his grandfather found silent films a weekend treat. He often took Bob and his cousins with him, and they would all stay to see the films several times at one sitting. After Federico's death in 1929, Bob's father, John, had partially filled the void by taking him to see silent films. In the theater, Bob felt no disadvantage resulting from his deafness. The subtitles leveled the playing field for him—it was like reading a book. For Bob's father, silent movies provided more than simple entertainment. The subtitles helped him improve his English, and he often encouraged his immigrant friends to go to the movies as well.

John also continued to instill in Bob a great passion for books. In his eyes, the Scottish immigrant Andrew Carnegie was one of America's greatest heroes. Carnegie had established thousands of free public libraries, which enabled immigrants to acquire cultural knowledge and to succeed in their lives. Maria also fostered Bob's reading. A gentle woman with common sense, she saw how reading could help him improve his speaking skills as he read aloud to her. Maria helped him control his volume when he spoke too loudly. She counseled him to go slowly and not to swallow his words. She encouraged him to feel his voice in his chest as he read aloud from a schoolbook or a novel. Like an orchestra conductor, she raised or lowered her palms to coach him in heightening or lowering his pitch and intonation. Gradually, Bob learned to "feel" his speaking voice and modulate the sound accordingly. His mother was a "loving drill sergeant," as Bob remembered her.

Within a few years, Bob's sister, Eleanor, nine years younger, was also offering him advice on his pronunciation. When Bob tried to speechread his parents, she would watch attentively and sometimes help him by repeating the messages. Bob was not

Maria, Bob's sister Eleanor, John, and Bob in 1939.

yet able to read lips well, and the best he could hope for during dinner was to understand only a portion of the conversations; he did this more easily when people spoke directly to him. Occasionally, a family member would write down something to be sure he understood. Bob soon learned to take an early leave of the dinner table and retreat to a book he had picked up at the library. This became his "tree house"—and the family came to respect and understand it.

Bob's peers at P.S. 103 all had normal hearing. Elementary schools in New York City were identified by numbers, not names. P.S. 103 was located near the Bronx River Parkway in the Upper Bronx. Not far away was the New York School for the Deaf at White Plains and also the Lexington School for the Deaf, but Bob and his family did not know about these programs. Most of his schoolmates and teachers accepted him as a "regular" since they had known him before he contracted spinal meningitis. As such, it was not too difficult for Bob to adapt and to hold his own. The fact that he had learned to read and write before becoming deaf was also helpful. While he did learn to read lips well enough to communicate with his friends, it became obvious early on that reading lips was useless in the classroom when trying to understand the teacher.

To address this problem, Bob's teachers would select a student to sit in an adjoining row and become his designated "helpmate"—a creative strategy, given that this was in the 1930s. Sitting in front of class with Bob, this student would write short notes or silently mouth whatever information was deemed important: a change of page in the text or subject lesson; what to copy from any special notes they wrote for themselves; important announcements by the teacher; and, of course, homework assignments. Bob did not feel self-conscious about this, only appreciative. His teachers would check on most of the details after class to ensure their accuracy.

Bob would never forget his favorite helpmate—a girl named Lily De Fiore. They were together for half of the seventh and all of the eighth grade, so they became a team of sorts. Lily knew his addiction for baseball, both as a player and a Yankees fan. She would often slip him notes—"How was your game Saturday? Get any hits?" Or she would hand him clippings from the sports pages about home runs by Gehrig, a shutout by Gomez, or a grand slam by Lazzeri. But despite their best efforts, Lily's notes, as well as those from other classmates, were not very helpful. Bob found it necessary to just focus on reading the textbook in class. When a *McGuffey's Reader* was used, which included many poems, he would hide the book and, regardless of what was being discussed in class, memorize whole passages of verse.

Bob's English teacher, Anne McGuiness, soon sensed his growing interest in literature and poetry, which had blossomed since he became deaf. She encouraged him to recite Robert Burns's "John Anderson, My Jo," and he pulled it off so well that when he returned to his seat, Lily De Fiore looked over from her desk and silently mouthed the words, "You're good!" In subsequent weeks, McGuiness had Bob recite "A Red, Red Rose," also by Burns, Joyce Kilmer's "Trees," Oliver Wendell Holmes's "Old Ironsides," and John McCrae's "In Flanders Fields." Seventy years later he would remember these readings "as though it were yesterday."[2] The admiration and acceptance that Bob received from his peers in school helped boost his confidence in classroom dynamics. Bob's classmates and teachers in elementary school saw the same traits in this young boy that made him outstanding as a teacher later in life. Another of his teachers, Rachael Sandowsky, wrote in his autograph book in 1934, "You have the rarest gift of all—a lovely and cheerful disposition."

If only all mainstreamed deaf children today could experience the caring teachers and understanding peers that Bob had in the 1930s. Without question, he had a lot to do with the establishment of this atmosphere of acceptance and support. His eighth-grade graduation book from June 1934 was filled with comments that reflected his full integration in the school. As Anne McGuiness wrote: "Good luck to you, Robert! I scarcely need tell you that I admire you greatly and that I am expecting great things of you."

After graduating from P.S. 103, Bob followed his good friends to De Witt Clinton High School, an all-boys program situated near Van Cortlandt Park and Mosholu Parkway in the Upper West Bronx, near the Hudson River. It was a good two-mile walk to school from home. The only times he took the trolley car or the El were on days when it rained or snowed heavily.

On the whole, Bob found the academic life at Clinton vastly different from grammar school. The system of rotating classes with fifty minutes per subject, along with ever-changing teachers and classmates, made for a fast-paced learning experience. There was less time for personal contacts, note-taking, and other forms of assistance from teachers. Classes averaged about thirty students. The exceptions were social studies, English, and literature—which were smaller, like those at P.S. 103. As the first year at Clinton drew to a close, the Great Depression was taking its toll on the family finances, and this became a constant topic of conversation at the dinner table, although Bob could only pick up bits and pieces of the discussions. Bob's father's business was struggling. Money was tight. People were losing jobs and going on the breadlines. Bathrobes, especially silk and smoking jackets, had become luxury items, and sales of women's housecoats, an everyday staple, were barely breaking even.

John Panara was a proud self-made man who lived the American dream of independence and hard work. He and his bachelor brother, Bob's uncle Ed, had made frequent business trips to eastern Massachusetts, which was gradually becoming a hub of textile manufacturing. They looked for a place to relocate their small business enterprise and finally decided on Fall River, Massachusetts. There they set up shop on the fourth floor of a warehouse. It was quite a challenge to move all the Singer sewing machines, hot presses, pattern-making tables, countless yard-wide rolls of wool, silk, rayon, terrycloth, and other paraphernalia dealing with the trade. Thus, the Troy Clothing Specialties Company was humbly launched in the very depths of the Depression Era, and the Panara family moved to a rented house in Somerset, a rural suburb across from Fall River.

With this decision made, there arose another challenge. What should they do about Bob's education? He was getting along well at Clinton, and all of his friends were there. It would not be fair to pull him away with the family move to Massachusetts. Bob wanted to stay at Clinton, too. Luckily, his parents found a solution—relatives. All three of John Panara's married sisters had families still living in the Upper Bronx. It was decided that Bob would live with the Bucco family—his aunt Marietta and uncle Joe, and their four children. The youngest, Connie, nicknamed Tootsie, was Bob's age—sixteen.

The Bucco family was more than a "second home" for Bob. Now he had a brother and three sisters. There was plenty of room for all of them because his uncle Joe was a prosperous building contractor and had built a large house. The family treated Bob just like his parents had. They let him be himself as long as he behaved and followed the daily schedule. As such, his remaining two years at Clinton went by without a hitch. In this second family, which was much bigger and noisier, Bob helped his cousins and his aunt and uncle to adapt to his deafness, just as he had done with his parents and sister. They learned how to include him in the small talk, the lively family banter, and the give-and-take discussions of personal problems, current events, and issues with relatives and friends.

Even so, Bob sometimes got lost in the rapid-fire conversations, and when this occurred he would retreat to his books.

As had been the case with middle school, Bob took on the responsibility of helping his teachers learn about his deafness and how to accommodate it in the classroom. In one required course, Elocution, he was expected to improve upon his inflection and speak with clarity, eloquence, and emphasis. He was also supposed to develop confidence in "public speaking" and impromptu talks. These were not easy tasks for a profoundly deaf teenager.

Bob took on these challenges, however, and his teacher understood his needs as a deaf student. Told that he sometimes spoke too loudly, not clearly enough, or that he had a pronounced Bronx accent, Bob compensated for these problems with a show of emotion and rhythm. And thus was born a presentation style that later brought him many honors as a teacher. In those days, there were no vocational rehabilitation counselors, and neither Bob nor his family had heard of the Fanwood or Lexington schools for deaf children located in New York. He had actually seen deaf kids signing on the subway in New York, but he didn't know what to make of it. He continued to focus on his hearing friends. With the personal approach of his teachers at Clinton, his deafness did not matter. He was praised for the way he handled off-the-cuff discussions, and he gained confidence in his public speaking ability, a skill that would prove essential later in his life.

The genesis of Bob's lifelong love for poetry and literature was fourfold. First was his need to find some sort of replacement for music in his life. Second was his passion for reading. Bob's personal reading choices, those not required of him by his teachers, often reflected the romantic and adventurous. From novels to poetry and books about the Wild West, he was highly involved in expanding his own learning while attending school—perhaps to compensate for what he was missing in class. He had a habit of carrying a supply of books around school, a bundle that always included a lot of verse. This was especially useful in classes where he had no help from note-taking friends. "For the most part, I literally read my way through high school," he explains.[3] Third, his mother had often encouraged him to read aloud with rhythm and pacing from the work of Byron and other literary giants. With these passages stored in his memory bank, he would delight his many friends, students, and colleagues through the years by retrieving these nuggets and incorporating them into his lectures and conversations. Even in retirement, these literary gems he had stored as a teenager would often surface in his discussions and enrich his conversations and presentations. The fourth factor was his supportive teachers. It was in Mr. Ferber's class during his sophomore year at Clinton, for example, that Bob recited his first passage from Shakespeare, a soliloquy from *Macbeth*. He read many plays by Shakespeare after that and became enamored with the Bard. Ferber impressed Bob, too, with his enthusiasm for teaching. He nurtured Bob's interests and often guided him to new reading material.

Bob had dabbled with poetry during his first few years of high school, mostly short verse on Valentine cards and those he penned during other holidays. This included secret verses to his cousin Tootsie's close friend, Geraldine, on whom Bob had a crush. Bob had never tried anything original or extended until his junior year of high school, when he submitted a poem to his school's literary magazine, *The Pelican.* In the foreword of a book of his own verse Bob published sixty years later, he wrote of his discovery of poetry while at Clinton:

> As the years passed and I progressed through high school, I learned to count the blessing of deafness in still another way. This came through the discovery of poetry and the realization that, at last, I had found that elusive nymph whose magic seemed to transcend that of her sister muse of song. . . . The sonnets of Shakespeare, the couplets of Pope, the ballads of Kipling—I literally devoured them by the day and hour, and then spent almost as much time listening to their muted echoes.[4]

As Prospero says to his daughter and son-in-law at their wedding in Shakespeare's *The Tempest,* "We are such stuff as dreams are made on." Having his first poem published led Bob to dream of writing more poetry. His family nurtured his interest in reading and encouraged him to write. Whether it was the subtitles of silent movies, the cultivation of his early love of books, or his experiments with verse as a high school student, language became the stuff that *his* dreams were made on!

Bob was delighted when he made the junior varsity baseball team as a catcher. With an enrollment of about twenty-five hundred, the Clinton boys came from a variety of ethnic backgrounds. Put together, many outstanding athletes emerged, and Clinton became a powerhouse in sports, often winning all-city championships in basketball, track, football, and baseball. The Clinton boys were addicted to winning. They often attended college games to learn new strategies. For Bob, there was more than just the pleasure of watching—like many of his classmates, he became a student of sport in addition to his academic classes. Clinton was also near the Jerome Avenue El, which stopped at Yankee Stadium several miles away. Naturally, when Bob and his friends played hooky on certain spring afternoons, they would elect to save train fare and to walk to the stadium. Good bleacher seats could be gotten for fifty cents, and if they arrived early when the gates opened, they could watch batting practice by both teams.

The Yankees being the "Bronx Bombers" that they were, many of those practice hits cleared the bleacher fences, so Bob and his friends often scrambled to wrestle for a bouncing ball. If lucky enough, they would have a brand new American Leaguer ball for their weekend sandlot games. During the Depression years, they had to make these balls last. When the balls became too scratched and torn for conventional use, the boys would peel off the horsehide cover, wrap tape around it, and use it for practice. For rival neighborhood games, they would all chip in to buy a Spalding—until one of them managed to come up with another Yankee batting-practice ball. Bob caught about a dozen of those American Leaguers during his high school years.

After the Babe retired in 1935, Bob watched Lou Gehrig's line drives dent the bleacher walls as often as they cleared them. "Gehrig was the undisputed RBI (runs batted in) king after the

Babe," he said, reminiscing decades later, "and he still has the American League record of 184 to this day, along with averaging the highest number of RBI's per game."[5] Having watched the "Iron Horse" throughout his years at Clinton, Bob was saddened to see him retire in 1939. His hero died of the spinal disease amyotrophic lateral sclerosis two years later, just short of his thirty-eighth birthday.

"Joltin' Joe" DiMaggio, the pride of all Italian Americans in New York, came along in the late 1930s, while Bob was at Clinton High School. Bob remembered him as "the best all-around player I ever saw; a great clutch hitter. Graceful as a gazelle, nobody patrolled the outfield like Joe." And it is no wonder that many Italians flocked en masse to see DiMaggio perform. The Bronx Bombers won four straight World Series from 1936 to 1939, and this helped keep management in the black during those Depression years while many other teams floundered in debt.[6]

Finding a Deaf Identity

After graduating with a New York Regents diploma from Clinton in June 1938, Bob joined his parents and sister in Somerset, Massachusetts, where Eleanor was attending a school run by French Canadian nuns. The Great Depression was still taxing family finances. Bob knew that going off to college might be too expensive. At the time, there were no government loans or state tuition plans, and the only other way to finance his education was through employment. Fortunately, there was the clothing business run by his father and Uncle Ed.

Bob began working as a stock boy, packaging bathrobes, smoking jackets, and women's housecoats. He also handled the yard-wide rolls of wool, terry cloth, and silk, checked the colors, and helped to load them in carriages and wheel them to elevators. For lunch, he went to his dad's office and ate sandwiches prepared by his mother. While his father took care of invoices and bills during the lunch breaks, Bob read the sports pages. His interest sparked in the sport of golf, he began borrowing his uncle's golf clubs to practice in the cow fields near his home. Those fields, bordered by quaint stone-wall fences, also became the baseball sandlots for Bob and the friends he had made over the past few summers.

Bob's father had no concern about his safety while swimming and often let him leave work on afternoons to go enjoy himself with his friends. It was at this time that Bob began to take up long-distance swimming seriously. He would row a boat while one of his friends swam alongside for half a mile or more, then they would switch. They did this at the oceanside beaches of New Bedford and Horseheads. Despite numerous times when people in the distance would wave their arms frantically to warn them to come closer to shore, Bob and his friends never feared sharks. A few times, the lifeguard swam out to wave them in—and lecture them afterwards. With Bob's love for the ocean, it was no surprise that he was especially enamored with the poetry of Lord Byron. Byron, who had a clubfoot, was also passionate about swimming. "And I have loved thee Ocean! and my joy / Of youthful sports was on thy breast to be / Borne Like thy bubbles onward, from a boy," Bob would quote from Byron's "Childe Harold's Pilgrimage." And like Byron, Bob "wantoned with thy breakers, they to me / Were a delight."

The poets Shelley and Keats and Bob's favorite novelists Robert Louis Stevenson, Herman Melville, and Ernest Hemingway, were also drawn to the sea. In an essay Bob wrote a few years later, he expressed his pleasure eloquently: "I love to stand at the bow of a sailboat when it is ploughing through furrows of dark green water, to sense the thrill and mystery of the boundless deep, and to tremble at every little thunderclap that comes when the wind whips suddenly into a slacked sail and stretches it taut."[1]

After a year in Somerset, Bob tired of his work as a stock boy. He began looking around for a place where he could study again. With his father he visited the University of Massachusetts in Amherst. There he met the dean, an open-minded gentleman who was willing to sit down with him at a typewriter and interview him in that manner. Bob responded well to each question, but the dean was concerned. He felt Bob *could* succeed at the University of Massachusetts but that his social life would suffer, and the dean believed that to be an important part of a postsecondary education. He asked Bob if he had heard about Gallaudet College. Most likely, the dean was familiar with the college, since the University of Massachusetts is not far from the Clarke School for the Deaf at Northampton. Neither Bob nor his parents knew about the college for deaf students in Washington, D.C.

Bob then applied to Gallaudet, writing directly to President Percival Hall, who responded by saying that he did not think Bob was ready for total immersion in classes made up of all deaf students. In any case, it was also too late for admission to Gallaudet that year. Bob had never met another deaf person his age, and he knew nothing about the education of deaf students. Hall felt that he first needed some time to develop a "deaf identity." He encouraged Bob to attend the American School for the Deaf (ASD) in nearby Hartford, Connecticut, for a year, mainly to learn sign language. Bob was disappointed, but he appreciated the fact that a man of Hall's stature had written to him personally and offered him advice. More important, Bob showed again that he could roll with the punches and make the most of each situation.

Bob vividly remembers how surprised he was that Sunday afternoon in September 1939 when he first arrived at the

American School for the Deaf. Deaf students were signing everywhere. It was a kind of culture shock for him:

> I couldn't sleep that night but tossed and turned in the throes of a nightmare straight out of Dante's *Inferno*. The next morning, I was resolved to pack my suitcase and quit the school . . . leaving Hartford for my hometown in Massachusetts. This had to wait until after school hours—and I still don't know what made me follow the Seniors as they rotated classes that Monday morning. I do know, however, that when I entered Mr. [Lloyd] Harrison's class in Social Studies something happened that turned my attitude around and changed my whole life.[2]

Perhaps subconsciously, Bob realized how in this new environment, too, one teacher could have a powerful influence on his life. He had many adjustments ahead of him. Until he came to ASD, Bob had been fortunate to have supportive teachers, but that alone would not make for a meaningful education. Much of his passion for reading came from his parents, but part of it derived from the fact that for years, self-directed learning had been just about his only option. Now, at ASD, Bob had yet to learn sign language. He didn't even know fingerspelling! He could read Harrison's lips and watch his teacher's eyes, but the tricks he had developed during his teen years at De Witt Clinton were only moderately helpful. Immediately, he became fascinated by Harrison's "windmill-like hands and arms—the language of body and soul."[3] Moreover, Bob observed that Harrison "made us learn without seeming to teach . . . he made us believe we could 'climb the highest mountain' and make it to Gallaudet College."[4]

With this initial level of comfort, he stayed on at ASD and became a "happy victim . . . of my teacher and my guide, who showed me how to communicate and teach the deaf and who led me to Gallaudet College."[5] Harrison repeatedly encouraged him to follow other people in "climbing ladders" to success. As Bob reflected years later, this was a time in his life when he learned that there were many people who made it a *habit* to climb such ladders. Lloyd Harrison taught him "the lessons of history, the stories and poems of our literature [that] offer many illustrations of the values of tradition. We can also learn much from reading biographies of men and women who never quit climbing, rung after rung after rung."[6] The indelible mark Harrison left on Bob was embodied in the words of the American writer Ralph Waldo Emerson that Bob discovered while reading several years later: "Our chief want in life is somebody who will make us do what we can."[7]

Bob also sought his "Deaf identity" during sojourns in the woods on campus behind the school. He found a location for peaceful respite, which he called his "Walden Pond," often sitting near a quaint log cabin, reflecting on his experiences in this new world of deaf people. The pond brought him much calm. "I finally came to terms with my deafness there," he reminisced, "and found my place in the great scheme of things."[8] Normally outgoing, it took months for Bob to immerse himself at least partially in school life. To some peers he must have seemed reserved. Others understood that he was overwhelmed at times as he adjusted to new forms of communication and learning.

During the afternoons, the ASD students took courses in vocational studies courses. Since Bob was there only for one year, he was not required to take printing, tailoring, or other vocational studies, although he did sign up for a typing class after a deaf teacher, Gordon Clarke, encouraged him with the explanation that he would be doing a lot of writing at Gallaudet. Among those who taught him fingerspelling and signs was Pierre Rakow, who was the media specialist at ASD and would eventually become a pioneer in captioned films. Bob spent a great deal of time hobnobbing with classmates, too, which helped him learn to sign with more natural fluidity. He picked up enough sign language to get along and to belong. He stole smokes with his new pals in the dorm stairways, sneaked away with them to go bowling or to see some movies, and even took off one night with them for a ninety-five-mile trip to New York City to see some burlesque shows. He also played a lot of intramural sports, but he decided not to join any teams since he knew his stay at the school would be short.

Another great teacher who inspired Bob at this time was Frederick Hughes, a deaf professor at Gallaudet College. In December 1939, Hughes was invited to deliver the main address during a celebration at ASD of the birth anniversary of Thomas Hopkins Gallaudet. Bob watched Hughes describe Gallaudet's founding of ASD with Laurent Clerc in Hartford in 1817. "I sat as one entranced, awed by the beauty of his sign language, the expressiveness and eloquence of this dynamic personality. It made a lasting impression and firmed up my resolve to go to Gallaudet."[9] Bob remembered Hughes's signs as much more than mere visual representations of words. They were brushstrokes, and this teacher was an artist. Hughes did not need to move his lips to communicate his message that day. His sign language and gestures spoke daringly to the audience, and Bob saw in the movement of Hughes's hands a life of its own. He began to wonder how such signs could convey the beauty of music and poetry. This was the moment when Bob realized the power of sign language to sway the mind and heart.

In the spring of 1940, Bob passed the entrance examinations and was accepted to Gallaudet College.

On the Carpet

Bob's ASD yearbook for 1940 described him as a "great dreamer," "which accounts for his talent for tardiness." He had adjusted well to the challenges of developing a "Deaf identity." He was even designated the class poet," and he wrote a tribute in verse to the school, which helped prepare him well for college. But a dreamer he remained as he entered Gallaudet College in the fall of 1940. His goal was to pursue an intense study of poetry. As he wrote in one of his student essays:

> My desire was to read poem after poem and book upon book of *belles lettres*. I had a plan all mapped out and by which I would first study the Classical writings of ancient Greece and Rome, next the works of the Renaissance artists, and from there continue on through Shakespeare and the Elizabethans to what I deemed to be the peak of all creative writings in poetry, the Romanticists. I was to be another Shelley and already I had decided to live the kind of life he had led in Oxford.[1]

Percy Bysshe Shelley, the young English Romantic poet, was rebellious and fought against political injustice. Bob identified with this. Like Shelley, he had a transformation in his life at the age of ten. The poet had been sent away to a boarding school

where the power of free thought led to his becoming a vision-
ary—and a daydreamer. Shelley, too, loved sailing, spending
summers at Lake Geneva with another of Bob's admired poets,
Lord Byron. Oddly, Shelley could not swim, and he died tragi-
cally during a sudden storm while sailing out to visit friends.
His final, unfinished poem was titled "The Triumph of Life."
Dreaming of being "another Shelley" was a radical path for Bob
to follow. Shelley, for example, was expelled from Oxford for
his rebellious writings. Before Bob could begin to even think
of writing anything, however, he would need to complete
Gallaudet College's "preparatory year" curriculum.

Many deaf students in this era came from residential schools
and were not fully ready for the rigors of college work. Bob's
roommates were Don Wilkinson, also from ASD, and Dan Van
Cott, who had attended a public high school in New Rochelle.
The Prep Exams, which had to be passed in order to qualify for
freshman year, were scheduled for the first Saturday morning
after the new students arrived on campus. The night before the
exams, Bob was so excited to have the opportunity to talk sports
and tell stories with his new friends that he ignored head senior
Frank Sullivan's reminder about the tests and his advice to get a
good night's sleep. A good mark on the exams would increase
their chances of being promoted to the freshman class, Frank told
the preps, and if they did well, they might even skip the prep year
entirely. The next morning, another new friend, Ed Carney, woke
him up for the Prep Exams. Bob said, "To hell with the exams!"[2]
He went back to sleep and never regretted the decision—for as
he would soon realize, the prep year would prove to be invaluable to him in adjusting to college-level work and developing
good study habits.

The obligatory hazing for preps at Gallaudet took the form of good-natured teasing. It included having to memorize an assigned name and being ready to recite it fluently in finger-spelling when any upperclassman approached. "From now on," said one upperclassman to Bob shortly after his arrival on campus, "your name is Benjamin Bergonsolus Benzogasolini." Bob liked this assigned name. The future poet saw it as alliteration with an Italian flavor. When older students approached him, he would obligingly spell out the name and be sure to dot the *i*'s with a pointed finger. The repeated action left him with the ingrained ability to spell his "name" more than sixty years later when he met older alumni.

A dramatic play was also required as part of the hazing, and the preps were expected to perform for the upperclassmen. In the fall of 1940, the war, then limited to Europe but threatening to engulf America, was on everyone's mind. On the third floor of College Hall was a large meeting room known as the Lyceum. With Bob as the director, the preps put on a fifteen-minute farce about the "Big Four" international leaders Franklin Delano Roosevelt, Adolf Hitler, Winston Churchill, and Josef Stalin. Little did Bob realize that this whimsical experience in dramatics, with his brief impersonation of Churchill, would foreshadow a career path in educational theater and literature.

One of Bob's biggest disappointments at Gallaudet was that the college had no swim team. Worse still, there was only an *unheated* swimming pool in "Ole Jim," an old building used mostly for basketball, wrestling, formal dances, and some meetings. The swimming pool had been one of the first things Bob looked for when he arrived. "It was useful only for ten or fif-

teen minutes at a time in May and early June!" he still recalls.[3]
College studies did not keep Bob from following his favorite
sports teams, however. After he had been in Washington, D.C.,
for only a few months, he quickly became a fan of the Washington Redskins football team. His fanatical obsession with the
Yankees never waned while he attended ASD. Now he and his
classmates would bet on the World Series games, with the win-
ners getting a free ride on an old horse wagon while the losers
had to take the horse "tongue" and pull the wagon. "The Yanks
won so often, I was always on the wagon with my Yankee cap
and my pockets full of quarters and half dollars."[4]

But with his penchant for "dreaming," Bob had difficulty
finding direction with his general coursework. As he wrote in
a reflective student essay the following year, "I was miserable,
and all because of the prescribed course of study that had been
forced upon me, especially the study of mathematics. I remembered how Shelley had hated this study at Oxford, and so my
hate doubly intensified."[5] Bob generally managed to avoid getting caught while committing pranks, including a variety of
youthful indiscretions. One night he and some friends enjoyed
a bottle of wine and subsequently removed the balusters on a
stairwell in his dormitory. On another cold night he and all the
preps, in their "birthday suits," were booted by the upperclassmen out of the side doors of College Hall and sent scrambling
into a huge snow bank, where they were rubbed down and
bathed in the white stuff. "We zigzagged back to College Hall
. . . up two and a half flights of stairs and into that shower room
to thaw out our frozen manhood."[6]

Gallaudet College, like many other colleges at the time, was still employing the Victorian method of discipline by "demerits." By the spring of his preparatory year, Bob had accumulated twenty-one demerits as a result of these offenses, perilously close to the twenty-five that would result in suspension. To make it worse, he was caught smoking in his room, which was a violation of the college's policy. He defaced his textbooks, cut classes, and openly argued with some of his professors. He once angrily tossed his math book out his dormitory window, only to have it land on the lower ledge outside the window of Frank Sullivan, the head senior, who returned it to him with a smirk on his face. Sullivan was probably not the only one who wondered if the prep from New York City would ever straighten out.

The turning point for Bob came one afternoon when he was led to President Hall's office, where faculty members were assembled and seated around a long cherrywood table. Irving Fusfeld, the dean, was presiding and began a round of questions, asking Bob if he knew anything about something that had been tampered with in College Hall. Hot under the collar, Bob admitted to having recently broken the stained-glass window of the Lyceum on the third floor of the hall while playing baseball with friends. He had kept his silence, being afraid to report it for fear of suspension. Bob saw several professors lower their heads as if to cover up smiles. Dean Fusfeld then excused him from the room, explaining that they appreciated his honesty about the broken window, but this information was not what they were looking for. Confused, Bob returned to his dorm room.

A few days later, Hall called a fearful Bob into his office. The president explained that they had learned that a janitor had broken into the business office in College Hall, and that the faculty was relieved that it was not one of the students. Dr. Hall turned to look outside his window and scan the wide expanse of Kendall Green. Then he faced Bob and said, "Beautiful spring day! Isn't it just perfect for baseball, too? But baseball should be played on Hotchkiss Field, Bob, not near College Hall, where the Lyceum's stained-glass windows make an inviting target."[7] Hall told Bob he would not ask for payment for the broken window. Nor would he add any demerits to Bob's already besmirched record, but the president was disappointed to learn about his immature behavior, including the math book incident. He had read Bob's poetry in the *Buff and Blue*, including "In the Realm of Fantasy" and "'Tis Christmas," and he had also read about Bob's hitting a home run in a club baseball game against Georgetown University the week before. Poetry and baseball were two of Hall's own loves. He asked Bob to think carefully about how he might be throwing away a unique opportunity to earn a college degree. Hall's caring approach to the problems Bob faced managed to turn the unruly student around. As Bob reflected, "This I did, and I gained a good friend for life."[8]

It was not just President Hall, however, who was concerned about Bob's study habits. Around this same time, Bob received a severe reprimand in the form of a letter from his father, who criticized him for his errant behavior and reduced his monthly allowance, which Bob could ill afford. It meant that he would have to curtail, among other pleasures, the number of major league baseball games at Griffith Stadium he could take in on Sunday afternoons. Bob dramatically recalls how his father told him that in the event that he was expelled, he would stop supporting him altogether. "One can well imagine the clouds of gloom that gathered around my brow then—replacing the laurel wreath that the fanciful Muse had becrowned me with only a few weeks before. Cursed be my lot, and cursed be the gods who had invented the geometric triangle!"[9]

Thus, summoned by the dean, admonished by the president, and scolded by his father, the rebellious Bob Panara, as he wrote in a reflective student essay, "had been weighed upon the balance of judgement and found wanting in good conduct."[10] Fortunately, Bob had been given one more chance, on the condition that he turn over a new leaf. "It was that time on the carpet with Percy Hall," Bob remembered, "that resulted in a reawakening as to what talents I possessed and how close I had come to wasting them, to disappointing Mom and Dad, and to not making the most of a college education."[11]

The Laureate of Kendall Green

Bob went from one extreme to another in his freshman year. He became involved in approved social activities. He was elected to various offices within the student body, and he developed a nearly fanatical case of loyalty to Gallaudet. It was like a switch had been flipped in his brain, triggering a new personality. He wrote several new poems that year, which his English teacher, Powrie Vaux Doctor, praised. "Doc," as everybody called him, compared Bob's writing style with that of author George Eliot. He especially liked Bob's essay titled "Diary of a Storm," an account of the hurricane that hit New England in 1938.

Doc was quite a character—a big, imposing personage whose booming, boisterous laugh and individuality infected everyone. As Bob watched Doc in class, he dreamed of emulating his teaching style, in which he exhibited enthusiasm, compassion, and flexibility. Doc became one of his principal inspirations. Finally Bob had found someone at Gallaudet College who appreciated his writing and who encouraged him to pursue it through every possible means. Born in Kansas in 1903, Doc, a hearing man, held master's degrees from George

Washington University and Gallaudet College, and a Ph.D. from Georgetown University. He had a deaf brother, which had motivated him to want to teach deaf students. He had joined the faculty of Gallaudet College in 1928 as an instructor in English and history, and he quickly became a highly respected and beloved teacher among his students. His dedication is exemplified in a story about the time his hometown friend Buddy Rogers, the movie star, came to the Gallaudet campus. Every student except one of the preps, who was in bed sick that day, packed Chapel Hall to see Rogers. Afterwards, Doc took Buddy up four flights of stairs to see the bedridden but no longer disappointed, student. That was the kind of teacher Doc was.

When the news of Pearl Harbor reached the Gallaudet campus on that tragic Sunday, December 7, 1941, Bob dashed upstairs to the Lyceum, where Edward Scouten, a hearing faculty member, was listening to the radio set and interpreting for an overflow crowd of students. Over the weeks to follow, there were many discussions in class about the war, mirroring the rest of America. Bob learned from his parents that several cousins had joined the service as the country responded to the surprise attack. There was nothing he and his classmates could do about the war, however, and with the renewed motivation he had demonstrated in the first few months of his freshman year, Bob continued to take his studies seriously.

Over the next few months, he worked on the metrical aspects of his verse, imitating some of the great poets he was reading. He had yet to develop a style of his own. By the spring of 1942, he had written "Nightmare à la Poe" for Doc's class, verse that offers the reader visual shivers of horror. In this poem, the protagonist lies "slumber bound" as the "pallid moon" casts its dismal light into his dormitory room. Two stanzas of this macabre work are provided below:

Lo, on the wall, how the eerie shadows float!
Lo, in that corner, how the evil demons gloat!
I saw the gruesome Guillotine
Outlined against the door,
And, on the lurid floor,
A corpseless head of nameless dread
That dripped with crimson gore,
That rolled in sickly gore.

Doc had given an assignment to write on the topic of dreams. That night, Bob was studying with his close friend George "Porgie" Elliott, who also loved poetry. It was well past the 11:00 p.m. curfew, and lights were out in all rooms. Bob and George brought chairs and small tables out into the hallway, where there was still some light available. There, Bob began composing. At the time he had been reading quite a bit of the works of Edgar Allan Poe, and his imagination was further influenced by the eerie tinnitus he suffered from. Bob finished his assignment around 2 a.m.

The next morning in class, he handed in his poem to be read and critiqued as usual by his peers and professor, seated in a semicircle. When Bob's poem finally reached Doc's desk and was read, the teacher's eyes lit up; he pounded on the table, and exclaimed, "Panara, you get an 'A' for creativity, and a '+' for imitating Poe!"[1]

Meanwhile, Eric Malzkuhn (nicknamed "Malz"), who was president of the Drama Club, made a radical suggestion that *Arsenic and Old Lace* be staged at Gallaudet. Frederick Hughes thought it would be impossible to receive permission, since the play was currently running on Broadway. Amused by Malz's idea, Hughes dared him to write a letter to Howard Lindsay and Russell Crouse, the original authors. Both Hughes and the Gallaudet community were stunned when permission was granted. Not only did the play run at Gallaudet, but it was successful enough that the cast was invited by Lindsay and Crouse to give a special performance at the Fulton Theater on Broadway. The show drew rave notices from the New York press. At that performance, members of the original cast, including Boris Karloff and Raymond Massey, sat in the front row and watched how the play was executed in sign language. It was the first time a deaf group had ever staged a performance on Broadway, and Hughes was a proud director that night, and equally proud of Malzkuhn, who had Karloff's leading role—and walked in Karloff's size thirteen shoes! Malz and Hughes had wanted Bob, a freshman, to take a small role in the play, but Bob was ineligible since he had just flunked his physics course. "I could have kicked myself for missing such a smashing hit."[2] Even though he was not an actor, Bob enjoyed his own brand of performance on campus. He was quite a hit at the informal socials and dances in Chapel Hall on Friday and Saturday nights. Known as the "tap-dancing poet in College Hall," the reputation came from his tapping up a storm on the hardwood floor of his dorm room to the point that occasionally other deaf students would come over to find out what was causing the dorm walls to vibrate. One night an upperclassman named Joe Stotts, who lived in a room on the floor below, flung open Bob's dorm room door and watched him practice his dance steps. When Bob looked up to see Joe, his muscular cow-boy friend signed, "never saw the likes of that in guys back in Oklahoma!"[3]

With Doc's encouragement, Bob developed more depth in his writing through such courses as English Composition, Advanced English, and Western World Literature. Bob's college verse ran the full gamut—some of it was humorous, some poignant, and some of his poems offered personal glimpses into his views on life, literature, learning, and love. He published many of them in the "Poetry Corner" of Gallaudet's *Buff and Blue* student newspaper. These included "A Soldier's Thoughts" (1942), "The Song Writer" (1942), "'Tis Christmas" (1942), and "The Charge of the Lucky Spade" (1942). These were in the days before television and rock music, Bob reminisced, when college students wrote and enjoyed poetry in general, and Bob was at the head of his class in this regard. In 1943, both the *Buff and Blue* quarterly literary issues and the Gallaudet Senior Yearbook included Bob's poetry. Once again he won the annual Alumni Poetry Prize. In 1944, Bob wrote "Of All Those Saddening Songs Sublime." In 1945, his last poem as a student, over 150 lines long, was a narrative titled "Thermopylae." Based on one of his favorite stories in Greek history, "Thermopylae" required a great deal of research for accuracy involving the names of people and places mentioned in the poem. In fact, he had worked on that poem on and off for a period of years, beginning when he read *The Iliad* and *The Odyssey* while he was a senior at De Witt Clinton High.

Inspired by the ancient Greek warriors who had laughed in the face of death at the titular battle, Bob began to research the story by studying books on Greek history. He wrote and rewrote that poem, studying another dozen books while at college, but he was not satisfied with the results until his senior year at Gallaudet.[4] In his poem, Bob detailed the entire battle, describing how Xerxes had led a special band of three thousand Persians (Medes) in the battle and how the Spartan king Leonidas and three hundred Greeks attempted to cut off the advance of the Medes, at odds of ten to one at Thermopylae, a narrow strip of land between the sea and mountains. When a local informer led a force of Persian infantry through a secret mountain passage behind the Greek lines, Leonidas was doomed with the rest of the remaining three hundred Spartans, all of whom died in the battle. A stanza from Bob's poem illustrates how he translated the information from primary sources into well-written verse:

> What use to him the prophet, what use to him the sage,
> What use are all the Magi so wise and keen with age?
> There is no man of Persia who dares his counsel bring
> When Xerxes stalks in anger and whips each living thing.
> For three long days thereafter, he watched the corpses mass
> As army after army was hurled against the Pass:
> The wounded fell to dying, the dead heaped on the dead,
> And daily, by the thousands, the brave turned back in dread.

For "Thermopylae," Bob won the annual Alumni Poetry Prize hands down.

The Significance of Reading

While Bob's passion for poetry remained undimmed in his senior year, he had realized that he could not emulate a life as fanciful and carefree as that of the poet Shelley. Everyone in the United States was preoccupied by World War II. Many of Bob's classmates were leaving college to support the war effort. Hundreds of deaf people were already in Akron, Ohio, working at Goodyear and Firestone, which manufactured parts and supplies. Many of Bob's friends were altar-bound, enticed by promotions and high salaries offered to people employed as war plant workers.

Although Bob had entered college with no ambition other than to earn a degree, by his senior year he was giving serious thought to becoming a teacher. Doc had insisted that he would make a good teacher of English, as well as providing a role model for deaf students. When Bob saw his classmates going off to support the war effort, he felt torn. He began to give serious consideration to leaving college early. In an essay for Doc's advanced English course that year, he summarized how, once again, the professor had come to his rescue: "I still don't know exactly why I am not wearing a golden wedding band. . . . Perhaps it was because, like Don Quixote, the gods on Mt. Olympus took pity on me and decided to exhort a Sancho Panza–like professor" to help him make the wisest decision.[1] Bob had written to "Burke" Boatner, the superintendent of the American School for the Deaf, who offered him similar advice. Bob's father, who greatly respected Boatner, also urged his son to stay in college and finish his education. He had more than once remarked how impressed he was with the "literary" content of Bob's letters home. It was evident to both his family and his professors that Bob had developed a strong foundation in literature. Still, he did not know what to do with it. Becoming a full-time poet was a luxury he had reluctantly forced himself to reject. "Thank God I listened to these Three Wise Men!" he said later.[2]

Lloyd Harrison at ASD and Frederick Hughes at Gallaudet were certainly inspirational teachers, but Doc showed a special ability to teach from his heart. A truly great teacher who brought out and cultivated Bob's innate love of English and literature, Doc "encouraged me to write, write, write—not only for his classes but also for the student publications The *Buff and Blue* newspaper and *Quarterly Literary Issues*."[3] Bob had become editor of both the *Quarterly Literary Issues* and the Gallaudet yearbook. Doc's encouragement to study the works of Shakespeare, Burns, Byron, Keats, Shelley, Tennyson, and the Americans— Poe, Whitman, Dickinson, Sandburg, Frost, and others had helped to develop the range and quality of his verse.

Even though there was no strong personal bond between Bob and Frederick Hughes, this deaf professor also had an influence on Bob's thinking about entering the teaching profession. "Teddy," as he was affectionately known to his Gallaudet students and colleagues, was much more than an ordinary teacher. He was witty and, to Bob's delight, a sports lover. For many years, Hughes coached the Gallaudet football and basketball teams as well as the track squad. Throughout his time at Gallaudet, Bob remained spellbound by Hughes's mastery of sign—his ability to combine sign language, English, and mime. Bob took all the economics and dramatics courses the professor taught and took every opportunity to attend Hughes's lectures onstage at the Literary Society meetings and in the college Chapel Talks on Sunday nights. When Bob thought about becoming a teacher, he aspired to emulate Hughes's magical style, using the whole bag of tricks in teaching the King's English to deaf students: motivating them to develop their expressive talents in writing, and taking it a step further by dramatizing their presentations of poetry and short stories onstage in the theater. Because of Hughes's influence, and his faith in Bob as a student, Bob believes all this became a reality.

Perhaps the most important piece of writing Bob produced during his college years was an eight-page essay titled "The Significance of the Reading Problem." This article, which began as a term paper for one of his courses and was published in the *Buff and Blue* in December 1944, brought attention to his potential as a leader in Deaf education. The scholarly discourse also fed his writing talents and fostered his self-confidence. More than any of his poems, this student essay opened the door for him to the profession of teaching. In it, Bob espoused his view that deaf people should "read almost twice as much as the average hearing person . . . in order to reap the maximum benefits."[4] Although Bob and his classmates had not been taught much about the history of Deaf education, notably the Milan Convention and the oralism movement led by Alexander Graham Bell, Bob was personally critical of the oralist perspective on teaching. Bell had been a source of conflict and anger in the deaf community. His advocacy in favor of the use of speech and speechreading in the latter decades of the nineteenth century and early decades of the twentieth century had not only led to the suppression of the use of sign language in American schools but also caused many deaf men and women to lose their teaching positions because they were unable to teach speech. "By directly attempting to teach the deaf to listen and talk like a hearing child," Bob wrote about the narrow perspective of the dyed-in-the-wool oralists, "we necessarily neglect other aspects of education, thereby making the deaf child even more unlike the hearing one."[5] Bob advocated the right of every deaf child to expression by means of fingerspelling and the use of sign language. "It is the most natural way . . . to understand the relationship existing between material objects and their equivalents underlying the printed word."[6]

Bob also discussed the need to carefully select storybooks and avoid difficult grammatical constructions, as well as "disquisitions that will prejudice young readers against the book and author."[7] Bob emphasized the importance of broadening reading assignments, for example, to include modern plays and good movie scripts and, where possible, "acting them out on the stage or in the classroom."[8] It was in the latter point of this essay that Bob first formally sowed the seeds of a teaching strategy he would eventually master. He argued that much time could be saved, and better results obtained, if teachers exercised their full creative powers with deaf children by *acting out* the narrative on the printed page. At least on this one point, on adding an element of dramatics to instruction, he was in accord with Alexander Graham Bell, and Bob quoted him at length:

> It is reading, reading, reading, that will give our pupils a mastery of the English language—it is the frequency of repetition of words that impresses them upon the memory. . . . Let the pupil spend half an hour a day in reading or spelling upon his fingers the language that describes a fascinating tale. Do not show him a picture, do not make him a sign, do not give him any explanation of the meaning until he has finished his allotted task. Then let the story be acted out and let pictures be freely used till he gets the meaning, not necessarily of the individual words and phrases, but of the story as a whole. He learns thus that the printed language of the book expresses a pantomime or a series of pictures. That it represents indeed a narrative that absorbs and fascinates him.[9]

In envisioning his own teaching ideal, Bob expanded this notion to include much more than pantomime with the printed words. He saw sign language through dramatic expression as a way to enhance learning through reading. Yet he also knew that he lacked experience. He saw the natural beauty in the expressive signing of his friends who were native signers, and he aspired to achieve this ideal himself, while developing his own unique style—in his words, "teaching that comes from the heart and soul, and not of the coldly conservative and somewhat reticent mind."[10]

Powrie Doctor considered "The Significance of the Reading Problem" to be an excellent piece of writing. It was a remarkable

summary of Bob's youthful conception of how he would like
to teach—*if* he were able to find a position. It was also, in effect, a direct plea to an entire profession. As he concluded, "If
we are ever to infuse the spirit of the Renaissance into the deaf
world of today, it would be well to take action now—they have
need for it."[11]

A month before graduation, Bob was offered a wonderful opportunity. Doc called him into his office and told him
the exciting news. Superintendent Charles A. Bradford of the
New York School for the Deaf in White Plains, New York, had
spoken with him on the phone and mentioned how impressed
he was with "The Significance of the Reading Problem," as well
as another of Bob's essays, "Poetry and the Deaf," which had
recently been awarded an Honorable Mention by the *Atlantic
Monthly* College Essay Contest. After Superintendent Bradford
came to Washington, D.C., and met with him, he offered Bob
a position as an instructor at the White Plains school. With this
hiring, Bob became the first deaf person to obtain an academic
teaching position at White Plains straight out of college. Previously in its long history, the school had hired deaf teachers
only after they had accumulated years of classroom experience.

Bob's family attended his graduation in the spring of
1945—their first and only visit to the Gallaudet campus. Rationing of gasoline during the war had made it difficult for
them to travel. Although Bob had demonstrated signs to them
during visits home, this was their first experience in total immersion with a large group of deaf people. The night before
graduation, Doc had taken them on a tour of Washington,

D.C. At the graduation ceremony, the proud Panara family listened as the "Class Will" was read, mentioning Bob's literary talents. Franklin D. Roosevelt had died just weeks earlier, and President Harry S. Truman personally signed the Gallaudet diplomas. Bob's class poem was also read to the new graduates and their families.

Sculptures in the Air

The summer after graduation passed rather quickly for Bob. He knew that it might be his last opportunity to spend significant time with his parents and sister in Somerset. Like all Americans, his family closely followed the developments in the war. As a student at Gallaudet, Bob had devoured Ernie Pyle's "GI Joe" reports from the battlefront, and he read of the brave battles led by Eisenhower and Patton. As a young deaf man, Bob would not have been allowed to join the army. Some of his friends had tried. Bob's roommate, Wayne "Tiny" Schleif, a hard of hearing boy who was a star basketball player for Gallaudet, had joined the army in the fall of 1944. He was one of the few deaf people who managed to make it into boot camp despite the government restriction against deaf recruits. His deafness went undetected until one night when he left the barracks after curfew. A sentry called out a question and approached him, but Tiny couldn't read the soldier's lips in the dark. Shortly afterwards, he was honorably discharged. Bob's personal heroes were the soldiers who were married to his cousins in the Bucco family. Since 1942, Bob had penned a series of poems about the war, including "A Soldier's Thoughts," "The

March of Time," "Our Next-Door Neighbors," and "We'll
Meet Again," One poem, "Aftermath," particularly illustrates
how his verse had matured:

"Peace!" the newsboys shouted loud,
"the battle's fought and won . . ."
  But the amputee lay
  in the feverish sway
of a war that had just begun.

"Peace!" the grimy G.I.'s grinned,
"arrived on time today . . ."
  But their spades gave birth
  in the desolate earth
to a hundred graves that day.

"Peace!" the cannons echoed nigh
and the flash lit every cloud . . .
  But the shell-shocked stared
  As the fireworks flared
and the nurses wept aloud.

"So this is Peace!" the sergeant cursed
as he finished his glass of rum.
  "Poor devils," he said
  and he rolled in bed
and he wished that his brain was numb.

The style now emerging in Bob's verse was one of reflection on people and events in his life. There was a very personal
quality to many of his new poems. As he waited in Somerset
to begin teaching, Bob wrote a final moving reflection on the
war, this one on Japan's surrender, titled "August 14, 1945."

One can envision the young deaf man sitting at the kitchen table at his parents' home that summer, watching his parents as they listened to the radio news reports.

> August 14, 1945
> They sat and listened to the radio,
> all hearts a-throbbing to the rise and swell
> of shrill discord from static Tokyo,
> from where a frenzied monarch tried to quell
> the repercussions of a quaking isle
> upset by force atomic. I could see
> the heart's rejoicing mirrored in the smile
> of every eye . . . also the memory
> of old abhorrence, of the primal fear
> which hardened into hate four years before
> when, like today, they paused and came to hear
> the first revolting echoes of the war
> and marched away to shut the doors of Hell. . . .
> I saw their tears salute the brave who fell.

Bob's poems on the war reveal an ability to write emotionally powerful verse. All six of them focus on the costs of war—especially in lives—but also in terms of the anguish about loved ones fighting in a distant land. In "A Soldier's Thoughts," the four stanzas probe the fears of a young recruit ("I'll never know if wars are just / Or whether wars are not, / All that I know who loves life so / Is that I may be shot: / A rosebud with no hope to bloom, / Predestined for an early tomb"). In "Our Next-Door Neighbors," Bob writes six stanzas about parents who, with a young son, Johnny, are filled with fear about his older brothers. They would often come to visit, apparently afraid to be alone with their own thoughts ("In that big house across the way / Where Johnny always wants to play / With all those model planes and guns / Built by two missing soldier sons"). In "We'll Meet Again!" Bob writes five stanzas about an optimistic lover parted by the war ("We'll meet again, we'll meet again! / Shed not a tear of sorrow, / For every war must come to end / Upon some bright tomorrow"). And "The March of Time" includes four stanzas—a Day, a Week, a Month, a Year—each described in terms of the life of soldiers away from home ("a Month / is thirty Yanks / trudging up a gangplank; / every mother's son / is wedded to a gun / and thirty minds together / think as one"). Like the other stanzas, "a Month" contains a vivid metaphor, and it is the very heart of the poem. "The March of Time" was one of Doc's favorites. When Bob wrote this verse as a college student, he sat at his desk, reminiscing about when he was young and his mother, like many Americans who were at first skeptical about World War I, shared with him the lyrics of Alfred Bryan: "I didn't raise my boy to be a soldier, / I brought him up to be my pride and joy, / Who dares to place a musket on his shoulder / To shoot some other mother's darling boy?" At the age of six or seven, he was her only child then. "During World War II, I realized just how mothers felt after that carnage."[1]

Many years later, in 1997, when Bob published his collection of poetry in a book titled *On His Deafness—and Other Melodies Unheard*, a number of reviews and comments were posted on the World Wide Web. In one blog on the Internet in 2006, Oscar Ocuto, who had just purchased and read Bob's collection of verse, called him "a Master Amongst Men . . . the e. e. cummings of deaf literature." Referring to "Aftermath" specifically, Ocuto wrote, "I'd like to share with you one of my favorites from this collection, since I thought it fitting, given the current state of turmoil in growing parts of this world. . . . The electric flow he generates through words, emotions and reminiscence sets one of many literary examples for the rest of us to draw upon." [2]

In Front of the Classroom

Bob's Gallaudet classmates remember him in their senior yearbook as a "scholar and troubadour . . . with a penchant for Romanticism." The "heart and soul" had begun to show in his own compositions. Gone was his dream of a life like Shelley's. Indeed, the world that Shelley had known had been destroyed. The United States was emerging from World War II. His family had not yet recovered from the Great Depression. Bob was deaf, without any savings, and about to begin his new position at the White Plains school. He would have to pursue his literary dreams in other ways. Although he had found his passion in teaching, he had only just begun to find his purpose. It is not surprising that his "penchant for romanticism" led him to Emily Dickinson, however. Her verse consoled him and reminded him that there were impressive libraries nearby in New York City: "There is no Frigate like a Book / To take us Lands away, / Nor any Coursers like a Page / Of prancing Poetry." Bob's own poem "In the Library," which he wrote while a college student, is a rhythmic tribute to his lifelong love for books:

This is the palace whose pleasures impart
The wonders of nature, the beauties of art;
Here are more riches dearer than gold,
Here lies more wealth than the kings knew of old.

Here is the wisdom, the craft and the lore,
Here are the whims of the wise men of yore;
Here are the visions for those who would dream
To rocket through space on a laserlike beam.

Here is the fervor, here is the love,
Here is the hope sought of heaven above;
Here is the laughter, the sweat and the tears,
Here are the songs that the world endears.

Here are the blooms and the blossoms of spring,
The cry of the loon and the lark on the wing;
Here is the vista of mountain and sea
Here is my sunny little Isle of Capri.

Here I'll meet sorrow, here I'll touch pain,
Here I can sigh for my lost loves again;
Here I'll greet pleasure, here I'll kiss joy,
Here I can dream like a seven-years boy.

Over this volume, over that tome
Wend all the roads that will lead me to Rome;
Under this alcove, deep in that nook
There I'll seek kismet . . . for there lies a *book!*

The New York School for the Deaf at White Plains, where
Bob began teaching in the fall of 1945, was close to home in
more ways than one. It was less than an hour from Yankee Stadium and the neighborhood where he had grown up. The

school was also in the heart of the Hudson River Valley, near the birthplace of author Washington Irving, of Rip Van Winkle fame. Perhaps this was apropos, for there Bob experienced awakenings of his own—a further maturation in his poetry, a discovery of his ability as a teacher to inspire deaf students in theater and writing, and, especially, romantic adventure with a lovely young woman from St. Louis—Shirley Fischer.

The school was only a train ride away from Broadway theaters and city universities. Known for many years as the "Fanwood School," the appellation was a shortened version of "Fanny's Woods," a name given to property in Manhattan where the school once stood. "Fanny," the daughter of a former superintendent, used to love to romp in the woods towering near the old school building, and the area became known as "Fanny's Woods," then eventually the "Fanwood School." Although the superintendent's daughter and the old campus were long gone, this nickname had carried over to the new location at White Plains. This was a residential military school, and at the time Bob began teaching, enrollment was restricted to boys. Bob lived in a mansion rented out by the wife of a man who had committed suicide after the stock market crash in 1929. The Fanwood principal, Justin Dozier, also had a room there. There were other boarders, including three who worked on Wall Street, a civil engineer, and a high school teacher. The housekeeper, Mrs. Cleary, made breakfast for them each morning before Dozier drove Bob to the campus.

At the Fanwood School, the boys in the primary department learned through the oral method, with an emphasis on speech and speechreading, while the boys in the advanced department used the combined method, which included sign language and speech together. Bob taught high school English, American history, literature, and algebra. When he began, the handsome twenty-five-year-old was unsure about how he would teach. His ideas about combining elements of drama might work in literature and history, and even English, but what about the dreaded algebra? While algebra had been his nemesis in high school and college, however, he learned after the first month that the deaf students were generally adept at mathematics. He merely had to stay one or two units ahead of them.

Unlike his year at ASD and his experience at Gallaudet, where he communicated with classmates and teachers while immersed in learning sign language and developing the "Deaf identity" President Hall had encouraged him to pursue, Bob was now responsible for teaching a group of young deaf people. Some of the kids reminded Bob of himself when in high school. They didn't know much sign language and were relying on lip movements. Some had been educated in Fanwood's oral program in their early years. Others were from deaf families or had been signing throughout their childhood. Bob remembered how his hearing friends at De Witt Clinton varied in their motivation, abilities, and interests, but this factor of deafness added immensely to the diversity he faced in the classroom. The reading and writing skills of his students also covered a wide range. Teachers in the field of educating deaf students have always been challenged by the difficulties of deaf students in learning to read on a level comparable to hearing students of the same age. Successful strategies for teaching reading have been few and far between. Bob had taken no teacher education courses at Gallaudet's Normal School. He had little time to think about strategies or teaching style. The primary focus during his first year was to find the best way to communicate with the entire class. And this he did with much spirit.

Bob's enthusiasm was especially apparent to students in the advanced English classes. So, too, was his love for poetry. Less than a month after he arrived at Fanwood, Superintendent Bradford asked him to stand before the school assembly. To Bob's delight, Bradford then read a letter from President Percival Hall of Gallaudet College announcing that the new English teacher at Fanwood had been selected as the first recipient of the George M. Teegarden Prize for Creative Poetry. When Teegarden's daughter, Alice, established the award in 1945, it was a foregone, but until that moment undisclosed, conclusion among Bob's Gallaudet professors that he would be the first recipient.

Among those at the assembly at Fanwood that morning was Bernard Bragg, a seventeen-year-old student in Bob's English class. Bragg was in awe that a deaf man could write poetry. In his own autobiography *Lessons in Laughter*, written many years later, he described his first class under Bob:

> We drank in with our eyes everything he signed. Using body language and facial expressions, he signed confidently and un-erringly, showing us that he was someone to be reckoned with and that he loved to teach. In contrast to the choppy, abrupt, and often homemade signs we normally used among ourselves, his signs were a miracle of vividness and eloquence. Most of the other teachers in our experience mangled their signing and kept their faces wooden. They also used language that was way above our heads, building a communication barrier between us. Mr. Panara established immediate rapport with us because he was one of our own and could communicate with us in our own language, sign language.

But above all, what electrified and enthralled us about Mr. Panara was his very embodiment of living, breathing revelation of the potential of sign language. Before we met him we had never realized that this, our native language, could be such a powerful vehicle for expressing the richest and subtlest feelings and conveying nuances of meaning as sophisticated as those of the most articulate English speakers and writers.[1]

Attributing to Bob his future success as an actor "largely because Mr. Panara was the first to encourage what was and is best in me,"[2] Bragg claimed Bob was the one who "awakened my literary and theatrical enthusiasms."[3] Bragg's tribute indicates that Bob wasted no time after arriving at Fanwood in developing a style of teaching that was revolutionary, overshadowing the fact that he was not a native signer. Internalizing the characters in the stories, he created a truly dramatic effect that captivated Bragg and his classmates. Bragg described Bob's emphasis on the meaning of rhythm and meter. The young teacher did this by tapping his feet and "drawing sculptures in the air" with his hands.[4] Bob would sometimes devote an entire hour to explaining a single stanza of a poem, "illustrating in sign the meaning of each word and phrase with unusual clarity, providing as it were a graphic and visual interpretation of the poem."[5] He described the plots of plays by Shakespeare, Aeschylus, or Eugene O'Neill, and the novels of Hawthorne, Dumas, and other writers, while vividly portraying the principal characters.

As Bragg reflected, Bob's "technique was not so much to describe as to enact."[6] When discussing that part of the story of *Cyrano de Bergerac,* in which the hero duels with the marquis who taunted him for his long nose, for example, Bob would parry and thrust with an imaginary rapier. Bragg continued:

> He caught and held our attention not just because of the lucidity of his signing but because of his evident love and enthusiasm for literature. At the same time he taught us something about English, until then a strange second language to us native signers, by interpreting in sign not just the overall meaning but every individual word in lines of poetry, of quotations from plays, thus making them finally come alive for us. I always entered his class with eager anticipation. . . . To see him was, for me, to experience a continuous journey of discovery.[7]

Bernard Bragg's description of Bob's "sculptures in the air" in his first year of teaching was particularly interesting, as it was the characteristic that many of his later students also admired. Long after American Sign Language had been established as a true language and linguists had analyzed its complexity, Bernard looked back at this new light on the language: Bob "injected a bountiful supply of ASL elements into his English-like signing, thus making his teaching of great literature all the more dramatic and enlightening. That kind of expression helped me to see English in its entirety; better yet, to fuse both thought and language at once."[8] Poetry and drama became "alive and breathing" for Bernard through Bob's unique style of expression.

The Fanwood boys, in their military uniforms, were no strangers to rhythm. They would go through their silent counting drills when on parade. Bob watched them compete with such schools as Culver Military Academy and Valley Forge, and the young deaf men would come away with many trophies for their marching skills. Bob also accompanied the boys to nearby West Point, where they saw the famed "Long Grey Line" perform their spectacular drills.

The Fanwood students alternated between vocational courses and academic courses, and Bob usually taught one group for three hours in the morning and another group for three hours in the afternoon. He found that the students seemed to grasp mathematics readily. He also taught history and health. He particularly liked having a significant block of time with the students. In his words, it was like the Little Red Schoolhouse. He followed his students closely and was proud to see many from his first class go on to Gallaudet College. He sensed that such students as Bernard Bragg, Allan Sussman, Suleiman Bushnaq, and Eugene Bergman would someday make names for themselves as distinguished Gallaudet faculty whose scholarship was exemplary. It was Bob's chance to practice what he had learned from Mr. Ferber at De Witt Clinton, Lloyd Harrison at ASD, and Doc at Gallaudet. And these young men proved him right. Bragg became a legendary actor, playwright, and educator. Sussman served as dean of student affairs and published extensively as a pioneering deaf psychologist; and Bushnaq was a professor in the Department of Business Administration. Bergman, who earned his Ph.D. in English, became a distinguished writer.

Indeed, his students sensed Bob's power to influence their future as well. Bergman later reminisced about his days at Fanwood:

> At the time it still used to be a military-style school for boys only and we all had to wear uniforms and perform drills carrying bogus rifles. The teachers were either old hearing ladies or

potbellied Deaf men. Against that background, Mr. Panara, as we all called him, stood out. He was tall, dark, and handsome like a movie star and always wore a pressed suit and tie that fitted him perfectly

But above all, what distinguished him was the passion with which he taught his subjects, English and literature, and the smooth, lucid, and artistic style of his signing, so unusual in a school for the Deaf where we boys used signs dealing with the basic human drives. He was a phenomenon, and we knew it. From him I learned how beautiful and rich sign language can be and how it can be used to convey abstract ideas. I thought to myself, if only there were more inspired and capable teachers like Mr. Panara in schools for the Deaf, how much better these schools would be.

Bob had the time of his life during that first year of teaching at Fanwood. As the first deaf teacher to begin at this school with no prior experience in the field of educating deaf students, he quickly showed his colleagues that he was well read and had unique talents in the classroom. Before starting there, he had been warned by some deaf friends that he was due for a rude awakening. They told him that the all-boys school was full of rowdies, tough kids from Brooklyn and the Bronx. Being born and raised in the "Big City," and going to an all-boys high school to boot, Bob had no qualms. "I was right. Mostly, they were 'angels with dirty faces'—but even the 'dirt' was missing as they were drilled like true cadets, washed and scrubbed clean, in pressed and natty uniforms, and [they], for the most part, saved their 'violent ways' for the gridiron, baseball field, and basketball court."[9]

On His Deafness

As Bob's first year at Fanwood drew to a close in the spring of 1946, he sat alone in his room one Friday evening and reminisced about his college days. Opening his copy of Elizabeth Drew's *Discovering Poetry,* he thought about a Christmas evening in 1944 when Professor Powrie Vaux Doctor had bequeathed one of his favorite books to him.[1] Bob turned to the front of Drew's book and read Doc's inscription:

My dear Bob,

During the past twenty years I have found only one student who thoroughly enjoyed poetry as much as I do, and, being somewhat familiar with history, I don't expect to find any during the coming twenty years, so I want to give this book from my library to that one student with the hope that he will enjoy this book as much as I did when I first read it in 1933 when the book was first published. Who knows—someday Bob Panara may take down some thin paper and write a little poem call'd St. Agnes' Eve.

In writing about "St. Agnes' Eve," Doc was referring to a letter reproduced above his own note on the same page. It was written by John Keats to his brother George and dated February 24, 1819: "Nothing worth speaking of happened at either place. I took down some thin paper and wrote on it a little poem call'd St. Agnes' Eve."

Now on this Friday evening at the Fanwood school after a hard week of teaching classes, Bob penned *his* own verse. The spirit of Doc was with him as he captured his worldview in the poem he titled "On His Deafness":

My ears are deaf, and yet I seem to hear
Sweet nature's music and the songs of man,
For I have learned from Fancy's artisan
How written words can thrill the inner ear
Just as they move the heart, and so for me
They also seem to ring out loud and free.
In silent study, I have learned to tell
Each secret shade of meaning, and to hear
A magic harmony, at once sincere,
That somehow notes the tinkle of a bell,
The cooing of a dove, the swish of leaves,
The raindrop's pitter-patter on the eaves,
The lover's sigh, the thrumming of guitar—
And if I choose, the rustle of a star!

"Imagination bodies forth," William Shakespeare once observed in *A Midsummer Night's Dream*. Bob sensed from the moment he finished the draft that the poem held a powerful personal message. A few days later, he mailed the verse to Doc, who was then associate editor of the *American Annals of the Deaf*. Doc loved the poem, as did Elizabeth Peet, a Gallaudet professor, poet, and coeditor of the *Annals* under editor Leonard M. Elstad, then president of Gallaudet College. The publication of "On His Deafness" in the *Annals* introduced Bob Panara to an international audience of educators.[2]

According to Bob, "On His Deafness," was partly inspired by John Milton's "On His Blindness," which was often in the back of Bob's mind. Milton, who became blind late in life, meditates on "this dark world," considers how his "light is spent," and expresses frustration that he cannot serve God as well as he would like. He concludes, though, that what is valued is the ability to tolerate whatever God asks, faithfully and without complaint. As the famous last line declares, "They also serve who only stand and wait." While Milton has a distinct religious element in his poem, however, Bob's verse explores the transcending power of nature.

The message in Bob's poem for both deaf and hearing people is one about how deaf people "hear" with an "inner ear" of imagination. Or as John Keats had written, "Heard melodies are sweet, but those unheard are sweeter." In this sense, Bob tapped into his own experience as a high school student. "You don't have to be deaf to know 'how words can thrill the inner ear,'" he once told a reporter, "but because of the way the deaf have been either purposely or inadvertently segregated from the hearing population, few . . . know how words can also thrill the eye."[3]

"On His Deafness" demonstrated intense visual imagery. In this poem, Bob employs onomatopoeia, or the formation of words imitating sounds, which was also a characteristic of some of the verse by Ralph Waldo Emerson, as well as e. e. cummings and W. H. Auden. The "tinkle" of a bell, "swish" of leaves, "pitter-patter" of raindrops, and "thrumming"of guitar strings are examples of the sounds *his* imagination bodies forth.

"On His Deafness" incorporates Alexander Pope's notion that "the sound should be an echo of the sense." When expressed in sign-mime, the verse illustrates Archibald MacLeish's dictum that "A poem should not mean / But be." Bob's poem is indeed masterful, and over the years it has often been brought to life in sign and dance by other professionals.

Some have enjoyed the print version best; others the signed poem. "I had read the poem three times before seeing it signed," Marilyn Darch, a freelance writer from Buffalo wrote, "and it didn't move me. I see it signed, and it gives me goose bumps."[4] Interestingly, Darch was not a signer. She had attended Bob's workshop "Poetry in Motion" in 1981, and her response was quite different from that of the many who were first moved by the original verse in English, and later equally impressed with the signed version.

The "rustle of a star" in this poem has still another metaphor. In the sixteenth century, there was a group of seven poets known as the "Pléiade," or "seven stars of French poetry." Two of them, Joachim Du Bellay and Pierre de Ronsard, were deaf. In *Divers Jeux Rustiques*, Du Bellay wrote a long tribute to his dear friend Ronsard, one deaf poet to another. Unlike many of his references to how his deafness saddened him, this "hymn" praises deafness and views sensory loss as a companion to be treated with humor. "Thou has with thee for companion gentle deafness," he wrote to Ronsard, "who commandeth silence, and taketh care that noise / Comes not near to hinder the joy of thy work. . . . In being thus deaf One is deprived of little good and much ill."[5]

The last line of Bob's poem "On His Deafness" has left a special impression through the years. Lou Fant, the famed interpreter and National Theatre of the Deaf actor, writer, and educator, dedicated his first book, *Say It with Hands* (1964), "To all those who have heard 'the rustle of a star!'"[6] Since 1946, "On His Deafness" has been reprinted in many books and periodicals and featured in signed performances worldwide by the National Theatre of the Deaf. In 1988, Bob's best-known poem won the World of Poetry's $1,000 Grand Prize. He gave the money to the Robert F. Panara Scholarship Fund at NTID.

In this poem Bob shows that an experience intended for someone—in his case, deafness—will find that person if it is meant to happen. One need not go in pursuit of it. He had found his oneness with nature and humanity and brilliantly expressed it through metaphorical verse.

Go with Your Heart

Shortly after Bob began teaching at Fanwood, he applied for admission to the New York University Graduate School in the College of Arts and Sciences. Doc had discussed the possibility with Bob while he was a student at Gallaudet, and Bob, taking life one step at a time, looked to such further study as a natural course of action. The chairperson of the NYU department was Homer Watt, a noted Shakespearean scholar and a wise and witty gentleman. At Bob's first meeting with Dr. Watt, he encountered a major stumbling block. Dr. Watt told Bob that he had never heard of Gallaudet and that even though Bob had excellent grades, the college had not yet received accreditation. He could not possibly give him equivalent credit without some kind of verification. He challenged Bob to give him samples of his writing. Fortunately, Bob had saved his term papers, publications in the literary quarterly *Buff and Blue,* and other essays he had written for his Gallaudet courses. Since he had served as editor of the yearbook and as a sportswriter and had published numerous articles and poems before he graduated from Gallaudet, he was well prepared to submit a portfolio.

Watt was impressed and gave Bob the option of enrolling as a graduate student with the agreement that he would maintain at least a B average, or otherwise take two undergraduate courses in English. Bob accepted this compromise and elected to take the challenging graduate courses while working full-time at Fanwood. He had a cousin with an apartment in Greenwich Village and stayed there overnight on Fridays while attending classes on Friday nights and Saturday mornings. His cousin Gilda, with whom he had lived while finishing high school, was married to a physician, and the couple loved music and often went out to jazz jamborees. It was ideal. Bob babysat their children on Friday nights after his classes and thus had a quiet place to study and a refrigerator to raid. He would then return to White Plains to teach on Monday and Tuesday, rushing to the city and back for a Tuesday evening class at NYU. The Tuesday night trip was often a terror. He had to take the train about forty-five minutes from White Plains to Forty-second Street, transfer to Washington Square, always worried about catching the last train back to White Plains in order to have time to correct homework and be ready for his Wednesday morning classes at Fanwood.

As with his high school education at Clinton, he had no interpreter in his classes at NYU. Interpreting had not yet become a profession. "I had to read, read and worry all the time. I probably read 3 times more than my hearing classmates, worrying all the time. That's probably where I lost my hair and maybe developed several ulcers in the process."[1]

Despite his new teaching load and now graduate studies at NYU, Bob kept in touch with his friends from Gallaudet, especially his former roommate, Eugene Schick. Gene was back at home in Indiana, dating a young deaf woman named Frances Tustin. Just prior to Bob's beginning to teach at Fanwood, Gene had shown him a photo of Frances and her best friend, another deaf woman named Shirley Fischer. Gene and Frances knew that both Shirley and Bob were Catholic and might make a good match. The duo figured it was worth a try. Bob found the young woman in the photo attractive and began corresponding with her during the year. As Shirley later reflected, "The first letter I got from Bob almost floored me! Even my parents thought it was pretty 'deep'. Quite a few "'ten dollar words,'" my Dad said, and very formal English—like an English professor. But, I liked his photo and he seemed interesting and honest."[2] As a young woman who loved to read, Shirley was impressed that Bob was a teacher. After writing again, however, she had to admit that she was relieved when his letters became less formal.

The woman who would prove to be the love of Bob's life, Shirley Marie Fischer, had been born on June 23, 1923, in St. Louis, Missouri. Her father was a World War I veteran and a lapsed Lutheran who had married into a very Catholic family and was willing to allow his children to be raised accordingly. Their first child, Edward, had been born three years earlier. When Edward was four and Shirley one and a half, both were stricken with the dreaded scarlet fever. Although Edward escaped with a mild hearing loss that did not prevent him from functioning in the hearing world, Shirley was left profoundly deaf. Her parents arranged for her to be educated, first at St. Joseph Institute for the Deaf, and then at the Central Institute for the Deaf (CID), both in that city. Both schools emphasized speech and lipreading, and Shirley did not know how to use sign language. After she graduated from CID in 1940, her parents enrolled her at St. Elizabeth Academy, a Catholic high school for girls. Since the school was run by the order that Shirley's Aunt Monica, a nun, belonged to, it was an obvious choice. She and Frances Tustin had known each other since first grade at the St. Joseph Institute and were like sisters. They even lived together in the Fischer home in St. Louis for several summers during their teen years. They also worked together as dishwashers at a Dairy Queen shop, and in a match factory.

The classes at St. Elizabeth's were hard work for Shirley. She substituted a typing class for Latin when she found it difficult to read lips when communicating with the nuns, whose habits almost totally covered their faces. After three months, she also dropped a course in shorthand, not an easy course for a deaf person, and substituted it with an introductory business course, developing some accounting and bookkeeping skills. She also volunteered her time in the school library, for the American National Red Cross, and with the St. Louis University Volunteer Service. Through these activities she found great fulfillment in learning about other people, especially when visiting nursing homes and state hospitals. Always outgoing, she had no trouble making friends with hearing people around her.

In spite of her deafness, Shirley played the drums for the St. Elizabeth band. Her teachers and peers at first doubted that . she could do it, but she showed them she could. She could hear the deep bass drum and a few other instruments, and she developed a good sense of rhythm. The band played many exhibitions, including a parade in Independence, Missouri, and in Columbia, Missouri, a university town.

Shirley also was extremely athletic—so much that Bob affectionately referred to her as the "Babe Didrikson of the Deaf World."[3] Additionally, her father, Edward Fischer, was a good bowler and taught her and her brother, also named Edward, those skills. The younger Edward would become an outstanding bowler who won many trophies as an adult. Shirley, for her part, played on the St. Elizabeth varsity basketball team and became the captain, winning many games against both Catholic and public schools. She also played softball and was one of the best on the team. Later, after graduating from high school, she played semipro for two summers with the Silver City Seals (Silver Seal Soda Company), an all-girls team in the St. Louis Industrial League. This was one of dozens of women's teams that had sprung up all over the country throughout the 1930s. The movement would culminate in the founding of the All American Girl's Baseball League (AAGBL) in 1943. The film *A League of Their Own* would later immortalize this league of all-female teams. The league never established a Missouri-based team, and by the time Shirley relocated, she was a married woman. Never being able to play professionally was a regret, but Shirley remained an avid fan of the AAGBL for life.

Shirley graduated from St. Elizabeth's in 1944 and received a small scholarship to go to Fontbonne College for Women in St. Louis. However, this was during World War II and gasoline was heavily rationed; her father, an automobile salesman, had no steady job. Having sent their son off to learn electro-mechanical engineering, the family knew that college was expensive, and the Fischer family was unable to send their daughter to Fontbonne. Shirley had never learned about the tuition-free Gallaudet College at either CID or St. Elizabeth.

Instead, she attended Mound City Business College and, within two years, received her certificate in accounting and library science. She then worked in several jobs, including Schiller Photo as a business clerk, and then with the American Automobile Association.

Shirley had dated many young men from CID, as well as Dick Sipek, who graduated from the Illinois School for the Deaf and who played professional baseball with the St. Louis Cardinals for a short time. She was still living at home with her parents in St. Louis when Bob Panara entered her life.

In August 1946, about a year after Bob had begun teaching at Fanwood, Frances Tustin and Gene Schick were married. Shirley was her best friend's maid of honor. Bob, busy taking courses at NYU during his summer break from Fanwood, was unable to attend the wedding. This missed opportunity was a disappointment to both Bob and Shirley, who had been "courting" via correspondence for some months. However, after Frances and Gene returned from their honeymoon, they invited Bob and Shirley to spend a weekend with them at their home in Evansville, Indiana. Bob, who was still studying at New York University Graduate School, had to wait until he finished around August 18. He then took the train and arrived in Evansville first. The next day, Shirley arrived from St. Louis. Meeting at the airport, Shirley got her first in-person impression of Bob. "Tall, dark, handsome, with a pipe, he seemed a bit 'snobbish.' That was mostly because he and Gene used sign language and fingerspelled a lot to each other when they talked. But I soon found Bob to be a very warm person who laughed a lot. He never seemed to flirt . . . so that also impressed me."[4]

Bob was instantly smitten. Over the weekend, as the foursome went out and played, he and Shirley eyed each other. She remembered being extremely impressed by his swimming and diving talents. The couple also played basketball for a long time while Gene and Frances sat by talking or watching. Bob, in turn, was awed by how skilled Shirley was with a basketball, something she would recall with amusement decades later. And although Shirley was familiar with the sight of sign language from attending events around St Louis, she barely knew any herself. Between her years at oralist schools and her interactions with deaf signers, she was comfortable enough with the culture that Bob's now strong sense of identity with sign language did not bother her. Bob began teaching Shirley signs that weekend. The mutual attraction was a serious and mature one. Both Bob and Shirley had dating experience and had had "steadies," so they knew what they were looking for. Even so, Bob still surprised Shirley. When the time came for her to go home to St. Louis the following Sunday afternoon, they all went to the airport and walked toward the ticket booth. Shirley didn't realize it till then, but Bob had his suitcase in hand. It was summer, and he was still on vacation. She asked him why he had his suitcase, and he replied with a grin, "I exchanged my train ticket for a plane ticket to St. Louis —that's where I'm going!"[5]

Shirley was stunned. Bob had never been to St. Louis. He had only read about the Mississippi River town and the paddle-wheel steamboats. During his stay there for several days, the two of them got to know each other better. The communication between them was not always easy. She knew little sign language, and Bob was not as skilled as Shirley at reading lips. During one date, Shirley ordered tamales, and Bob, reading her lips, told the waitress he'd have the same—a Tom Collins!"

Enamored by this young woman, Bob returned to Fanwood and wrote a poem, "To Shirley," and mailed it to her.

As Bob focused on his teaching again, the attractive young lady in St. Louis occupied his thoughts during his free moments. He corresponded regularly with her and visited her when he could. At Christmas, Shirley stayed for a week with Bob's family in Massachusetts. Even though she was not Italian, his family loved her. Bob had to return to Fanwood two days early, however, and left Shirley with his parents. Within a few days, she demonstrated her own self-reliance by taking the train from Providence, Rhode Island, to Penn Station in New York City, then to White Plains, and a taxi cab to Fanwood, just in time to have lunch with Bob and some other teachers. She sat in one of Bob's classes and observed him. Then a friend drove them both back to Penn Station and they had a chance to hold hands in the back seat for a half hour before she had to head back to St. Louis.

On Easter Day in 1947, Bob proposed marriage to Shirley in St. Louis, while Fanwood was on spring break. He gave her a half-carat diamond ring, which he had purchased at Macy's with the help of his mother. Father Drescher of Pope St. Pius Catholic Church in St. Louis, where the Fischers were parishioners, married them on July 12, 1947. It was a Saturday morning, and the church was filled to the balcony. Bob's parents and his sister Eleanor attended, but many other friends had difficulty finding

Bob and Shirley on their honeymoon on the deck of the Hudson River Line, 1947.

transportation over long distances so soon after the war. Shirley's brother, Edward, who had married several years earlier and worked locally at a stove-manufacturing company, was also there with his wife. Following the wedding, there was a breakfast for the bridal party and the two families. Rather than resting up for the evening reception, Shirley then took Bob forty miles to the convent in O'Fallon that afternoon, where her aunt, Sister Monica, was residing. Other nuns there included Shirley's former teachers and they were overjoyed to see her and meet her new husband.

At the reception that night in a folksy German rathskeller, the newlyweds danced up a storm with their many deaf and hearing friends. Shirley always enjoyed relating what would happen next. As they left the reception and waved good-bye to their many friends, Bob's father-in-law handed him the keys to the car and, embarrassed, he explained that he had never learned to drive. He had gone to college during World War II and gasoline rationing had made it difficult for everyone to use automobiles. In New York City, he would either walk or take the train. Undaunted, Shirley grabbed the keys and in her wedding gown, got behind the wheel and drove off toward the hotel. When they arrived, the parking lot attendants and doorman could not keep a straight face when the bride pulled up in the car with the "Just Married" sign. Bob got out, blushed, and quickly escorted Shirley into the hotel, knowing well that the young men were having a good laugh at their expense. It was, as Bob recalled, "Life's Darkest Moment!"

Bob's parents gave the newlyweds a thousand dollars, and his dad offered him advice: "Bob, use the money to buy a car, and learn to drive!" As he was becoming something of a laughing stock among the teachers and students at Fanwood, Shirley told him in private, "I'll teach you how to drive in New York if you teach me how to communicate in sign language." He quickly took lessons from her using a new Chevrolet they purchased. He passed his driving test within a month.

Living arrangements at Fanwood presented a problem. Neither Bob nor Shirley had much money, and White Plains, home to many Manhattan-based businessmen, was outrageously expensive. Further complicating things was the standard practice of giving returning GIs first pick of the affordable prefab housing springing up everywhere. The couple turned to the Fanwood superintendent, Charles Bradford, about their dilemma, a decision that turned out to be providential. Bradford immediately offered the Panaras lodging on-campus. Their apartment in Peet Hall was small— two rooms with a bathroom in between—but the newlyweds were thrilled with it and delighted that their "neighbors" were other faculty members. If they missed meals in the school dining area they could heat up something in the shared kitchen area in Peet Hall.

Bob was greatly enjoying himself in the classroom. He now taught two classes in the advanced department, each for three full hours daily. History was fun for him since he had studied the subject in depth at Gallaudet, and he could often tie a history lesson to something that he also covered in literature. Because of the popularity of his literature classes, the students were delighted when Bob set up a literary society that met one night a month in the auditorium. The boys were in grades eight

Deaf students in their military uniforms at the New York School for the Deaf at White Plains, 1946.

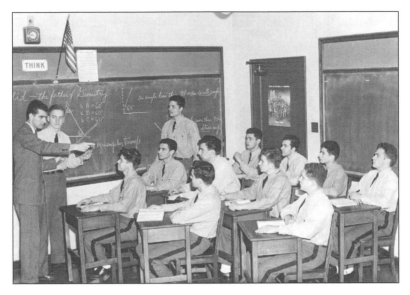

At the New York School for the Deaf at White Plains (Fanwood), Bob's teaching included, of all subjects, geometry!

through ten and were assigned either a short story or a poem to present in sign language. Sometimes they chose their own. Bob also set up a panel of judges consisting of faculty and seniors, and he established a rating system so that at the end of the school year, students would be recognized for best short-story telling, most promising poetry reading, and other honors.

Bob had generally shied away from the stage while a student at Gallaudet. Since he did not learn sign language until the age of nineteen while at the American School for the Deaf in Hartford, he felt somewhat insecure when he was among native signers. Thus, he never tried out for a role in the annual plays of the Gallaudet Dramatics Club, and other than the preparatory year skit, he had only on a few occasions joined his friends during amateur nights at the monthly Literary Society meetings. His friend Malz did coax him once to accept the role of the hero in the one-act melodrama "She Was Only a Farmer's Daughter."

Now Bob had created the Fanwood Dramatics Club and found himself directing plays, a new experience for him. Many of the students who had gained confidence onstage in the Fanwood Literary Society also gravitated toward dramatics. Two stage performances were presented yearly, consisting of one-act plays such as *Can't You Take a Joke?* set in an all-boys prep school; *The Bishop's Candlesticks* (excerpted from *Les Miserables*); and *Murgatroyd,* a humorous tale of mistaken identity. Bob adapted *A Christmas Carol* into two acts, and it was a big hit. The school's board of directors attended the second night's performance and loved it.

Although still a high school student, Bernard Bragg not only helped to direct, but he also took on the role of Scrooge, revealing the whole range of that character's emotions as he was led into Christmas past, present, and future. Prior to this performance, Bob had known that Bragg was a natural, but this interpretation convinced him that he would be a "future star of the first magnitude in Deaf theatre."[6] Onstage, his latent talents exploded, and Bob could see that this young man had something special to offer. Indeed, Bragg had an amazing talent for mimicry and mime, something Bob considered a fourth dimension to characterization and body language onstage.

Bob's ability to recognize potential and foster it through encouragement and inspiration was something he had learned from Lloyd Harrison and Doc. It was a characteristic he learned to cherish as time went on. The Fanwood Literary Society and the Fanwood Drama Club played a major role in helping a generation of deaf students develop communication skills, stage presence, and confidence. This experience, too, was to lay the theoretical foundations for Bob's later experimental educational theater.

Meanwhile, Shirley had quickly assimilated into the school culture. At the same meeting where he offered the Panaras on-campus lodging, Superintendent Bradford had suggested that Shirley become the school librarian. It was an ideal arrangement; she would not have to drive to work or struggle in communicating with coworkers. It also meant that she could have lunches with Bob. With her training in library science and her love for reading, she enthusiastically approached her new responsibilities. She overhauled the entire library, converting it to the Dewey decimal system. She scoured the basements and

Shirley with one of her classes in the library of the New York School for the Deaf at White Plains (Fanwood), 1948.

storage areas of various buildings on campus in search of old books, journals, and other materials, and refurbished the entire library to make it a true resource center. More important, Shirley encouraged the Fanwood boys to take more of an interest in the reading materials available. Every month during the year, Charles A. Bradford expected Fanwood teachers to present a program to the school's staff in an assembly. They were asked to choose a topic within the context of their classes, such as examples of the work they were doing or a story related to the course. Shirley asked to be involved in this professional development assembly program. Within a few months of marrying Bob, she had learned sign language, and she volunteered to put on a demonstration, "Know Your Library," which greatly impressed the school faculty and administrators.

Bob's graduate studies at NYU served to heighten his youthful passion for both literature and sports. One night at the first session of a course called "Emerson and the Transcendentalists," Bob sat in the front row and waited for the other students to file in and for Professor Nelson Adkins to show up. A young man sat down next to him, and Bob could not help noticing the length of his outstretched legs. With his usual lack of self-consciousness, he explained to the fellow that he was deaf and asked him if he would be willing to let him copy his notes in the class. While talking to the tall student, Bob suddenly realized that he was the rookie center for the New York Knicks pro basketball team. He blurted out, "You're Dick Holub, who played for Claire Bee at Long Island University!" Dick smiled . . . and agreed to take notes for Bob.

In addition, he gave Bob free tickets to games—seats right behind the Knicks' bench. On game nights, Dick could only help Bob take notes until 7:30 p.m., when he had to catch a train to make the warm-ups at the Sixty-ninth Regiment Armory at Twenty-fifth Street and Lexington before game time at 8:30. As he got to know Dick, Bob asked him why he was majoring in English at NYU. Holub told him that English was actually his first love. He had even written some poetry, and there was no guarantee, with his trick knee, that he could maintain a career as a professional basketball player. Furthermore, in those days the NBA was a fledgling organization, one that had yet to become popular with fans. In view of all these uncertainties, Holub planned to coach and perhaps teach English in the future. Although he and Bob eventually lost touch, that seems to have been his destiny. Dick earned a master's degree from NYU in English, a doctorate from Columbia University in 1961, and in addition to teaching English, served as Fairleigh Dickinson University's basketball coach for many years, being inducted into its Hall of Fame in 1999. Shirley was an avid basketball fan too, having played in high school, and she enjoyed the Knicks games with Bob while he was studying at NYU. They sat behind the bench thanks to the free tickets given them by Holub. Several times they took Dick out for dinner before class when no games were scheduled.

On some nights when Bob attended classes, Shirley would drive him to NYU and then park nearby in Greenwich Village to visit Bob's cousin Gilda. On many occasions, Bob and Shirley stayed in the city overnight and then spent Saturday taking in a Broadway show, the vast libraries, or going to see the Rockettes at Radio City Music Hall. On occasion, they would meet up with Bob's parents at the homes of assorted cousins in the Bronx. They also attended the Midtown Supper Club, an intellectual gathering of many deaf and hard of hearing people held in different restaurants. The club was able to invite guest speakers of note to these soirées, such as Eleanor Roosevelt, the novelist Edna Ferber, and Gallaudet's president Leonard Elstad. Shirley knew many of the regulars in that group, especially those who had attended St. Joseph's and the Central Institute for the Deaf in St. Louis, or those she had met in meetings of oral deaf people before she met Bob. Club members included Jim Marsters, who was studying in the NYU pre-med program, Martin Sternberg, Bill Bernstein, and the chemist Bill Rodgers. Some of them were committed "oralists" but would use sign language with the Panaras and other deaf friends.

In 1948, Bob became the first deaf person to receive a master's degree in English from New York University. His parents were extraordinarily proud of him. Bob felt that Shirley deserved a lot of credit for all her help and encouragement. Gallaudet president Leonard M. Elstad, who had replaced Percival Hall in 1946, sent Bob a letter:

> I should have written you before congratulating you upon receiving your Master of Arts degree in English from New York University. This is a very unusual event in the history of the education of the deaf. I rather think you are the first graduate of Gallaudet College who has gotten an advanced degree in English, which makes your accomplishment all the more remarkable. I hope that sometime you can come down and tell the student body just how you did it. They need a "shot in the arm" sometimes from those who have been here and know the difficulties.[7]

The two years in the Big Apple while Bob pursued his master's degree were a special time for Bob and Shirley. Foot-long hot dogs during the many walks in Washington Square would remain a fond memory. So would charcoal sketch artists exhibiting their handicraft. Another favorite experience was buying a poem for fifty cents from Maxwell Bodenheim after a poetry reading. Bob and Shirley saw their families as often as they could. During one visit from St. Louis, the Fischers stayed with them in White Plains for a week. Shirley's father, who loved dancing, took them all out on a Saturday night to Schmidt's Farm, where they bumped into his cousin Tootsie's friend Geraldine, on whom Bob had had a crush a decade earlier. Now Geraldine was with her husband, and Bob proudly introduced her to his beautiful blue-eyed blonde bride, Shirley, and her parents.

In 1949, Bob and Shirley were at Camp Mohican on Lake George in upstate New York, serving as informal counselors to a Fanwood boy attending the all-hearing YMCA camp. One day, there was a phone call; it was their friend, Superintendent Bradford, saying that an important letter had arrived for Bob. The ever-generous Bradford personally drove the missive out to the camp. It was a letter from Leonard Elstad, the president of Gallaudet University, offering Bob a job there. For Bob, it was an extremely difficult decision. In only two weeks, the college would open, and he would have to be there for the first day of classes. He adored the Fanwood School, and so did Shirley. He would have to leave the home of Washington Irving and Ichabod Crane, which he loved as much as his students, not to mention the exciting football and basketball games against Class A high schools. There was also the factor of being so far away from the Panaras, who were a mere three hours away from Fanwood. Torn, Bob and Shirley returned to Fanwood the following day to ponder. It took them a full week and considerable anguish to make the decision. In the end, it was the adventurous Shirley, who had never set foot on Kendall Green, who convinced Bob that he should accept the offer at the world's only college for the deaf.

"Go with your heart," she counseled him.[8]

Return to Kendall Green

Upon arriving in Washington, Bob and Shirley drove to Doc's big "House #7" on Faculty Row on Gallaudet's campus, the first floor of which he shared with his chronically ill mother. Francis Higgins, another Gallaudet professor, lived with his family on the second floor. Bob and Shirley moved into a two-room apartment on the third floor. Bob and Shirley had their daily meals with the other faculty and staff who had no kitchen facilities. It was a full house, but one that made them very happy.

As an instructor at Gallaudet College, Bob began teaching English. The *Buff and Blue* proclaimed him to be "one of the brilliant young men in the Class of '45."[1] Shirley also found employment as a part-time library assistant and worked for a while as a typist and proofreader for the *American Annals of the Deaf.* When she became a physical education instructor for women at Gallaudet, coaching both the women's bowling and basketball teams, everyone quickly learned that she had as much fighting spirit as her husband. While coaching the varsity women's basketball team, the "Gallaudet Co-Ednas," Shirley learned that the girls were not allowed to practice in Ole Jim in the afternoon because the men's team had priority. The women's team was forced to practice in the late evening hours, after completing their homework, but this only made Shirley and her team all the more determined to play well. They went on to post a winning season with eight wins and two losses, facing such tough opponents as the University of Maryland, George Washington University, and American University. As Shirley reminisced, "This achievement was made doubly sweet in view of the fact that the men's varsity finished the season with only four wins against 11 losses."[2]

Shirley won many trophies in individual and team bowling, including one for scoring 267 from scratch (no handicap). With encouragement from Milton Friedman, a sports leader in Washington, D.C., she also helped to establish the Eastern Deaf Women's Bowling Association and served as its first president. Those early years at Gallaudet were busy, all the more so when Shirley learned she was pregnant. On July 21, 1951, she gave birth to a son, John, named for Bob's father, who was delighted, and even more so that John's middle name was Edward, for Shirley's father as well as for Grandpa John's brother and best friend. Shirley had stopped coaching when she became pregnant. Given that Bob and Shirley had both been deafened by illness, it was no surprise when John proved to be hearing. The infant John learned quickly about Bob's baseball enthusiasm. One day in late September 1951 his father was holding him while watching the telecast of the Giants' one-game playoff with the Dodgers. When Bob saw Bobby Thompson's historic home run clinch the game for the New York Giants, he tossed the baby in the air, but luckily caught Johnny coming down as he let out a "shout heard around the world!"

Bob reacquainted himself with old friends, including President Percival Hall, now retired but still living on campus in the "Old White House" on the hill. Hall was the president who had helped Bob turn around when he lost direction in his preparatory year. Hall had lost much of his vision to age, but the gentle old man nevertheless enjoyed walking down to the snack bar in Ole Jim to chat with the students. After spending many afternoons listening to Hall's anecdotes, Bob wrote a poetic tribute titled "To Percival Hall, Our Mentor," comparing him to the aged Ulysses:

> Though you are left to play a lonely role
> Where all your days are spent in reverie
> Like one returned from some long Odyssey,
> Still must we marvel at your strength of soul
> Which drew its inspiration from an age
> When Kendall Green was in its infancy
> And Lux, such as we know it now to be,
> Was only for the dreamer to presage.
>
> Yet dream you did—and out of it ensued
> A life of high devotion to an aim
> Which swept the fancy of the multitude
> And brought our Alma Mater such acclaim
> That now, when all your deeds have been reviewed,
> Like Gallaudet, you have become a name.

Hall was so touched by the poem published in the Gallaudet College Alumni Association newspaper that he wrote Bob a personal note: "Some things happen only once in a lifetime. This is the case in connection with your poem in the Alumni Bulletin written in my honor. This has never happened to me before, and I appreciate it all the more because it is so well done."[3] Bob reflected, "It was the least I could do for my mentor and good friend."[4] Shortly afterwards, Hall's daughter-in-law told Bob that the former president had memorized the verse by heart.

Bob continued to teach freshman and sophomore English, a survey of English literature, and a survey of American literature, and his classroom became his stage. He built on the teaching style that had captivated his students at Fanwood, getting them to think on their feet, literally. He also continued to blend the best characteristics of his Gallaudet role models, Powrie Vaux Doctor and Frederick Hughes, into his own unique teaching style. Like Doc, he used signing with voice for some of his instruction, but like Hughes, sign and mime without voice for dramatizing and illustrating certain points.

Things began to change in 1952, when George E. Detmold was hired as dean of instruction. Detmold was asked to analyze the curriculum and propose changes with the goal of improving Gallaudet's chances for accreditation. He had earned his bachelor's and master's degrees and a Ph.D. from Cornell University, and as an "outsider," he was the subject of resentment by the Gallaudet faculty as he overhauled the curriculum. Detmold didn't like the dramatics course taught by Frederick Hughes, and he eliminated it. This was an odd decision from the perspective of some of the faculty, since Detmold had obtained his Ph.D. in theater. Hughes was so embittered that the deaf professor never again attended student plays by the Dramatics Club. Nor did he involve himself in any extracurricular activities initiated by Detmold. Bob took over as advisor to the Dramatics Club.

Next, Detmold implemented a Humanities Program that included requirements to study such works as St. Augustine's *Confessions* and Dante's *Divine Comedy*. The average Gallaudet preparatory, or first-year, student entered reading at a ninth-grade level, however, and the impact of deafness on reading ability was a factor that Detmold seemed to overlook. Despite Bob's own experience with Professor Watt at NYU, when he learned that Gallaudet had not yet been accredited, and his acceptance of the need for change at the college where he was now teaching, Bob felt that Detmold was going about it all wrong.

Detmold did promote Bob to chair of the English Department, and he moved Doc to chair of the History Department. Doc had learned to be cautious with Detmold. He was a pragmatist and basically went along without much resistance as Detmold proceeded with the curriculum changes. Bob, however, was angry over Detmold's choice of required readings, and he was especially angry with the way the deaf faculty were being treated.

It was about this time that Bob wrote his poem "Turnabout," sparring with a hypothetical professor in the classroom. It was published in the journal *College English*.[5] He was the first Gallaudet faculty member to publish in that prestigious journal.

> Professor! I must humbly interfere
> With this dramatic cloak and dagger view
> Of *Don Quixote,* in the guise which you
> Have brought to life this courtly atmosphere

Of old. I praise those sixty years and two
Which mark your learning and which somehow, too,
Have forced me to repeat the course this year,
And yet—I beg your pardon—but I must
Cross swords with you, though forty years your youth,
And, raising *Sancho Panza* from the dust,
Remind you of his day and age, forsooth.
For, I repeat again, my cause is just
It's fifty minutes after ten—
Hey, fellers, 'taint the truth?

Doc was delighted to see Bob have his verse published in *College English*. His former student had also begun writing a column, "The Silent Lyre," for *The Silent Worker*, a magazine for the deaf community. In this column, he highlighted the works of deaf poets. He also published some of his own verse. In 1954, he published in *The Silent Worker* a seminal article titled "The Deaf Writer in America: 1900–1954," thus laying the foundation for the literary component of what was to become the field of Deaf Studies. As Bob's scholarly reputation grew, the bond between Bob and Doc had grown stronger. When more space was needed to accommodate students as the enrollment expanded, Detmold asked the faculty to relocate off Kendall Green. Bob had found an apartment in Kent Village in Maryland and located a townhouse there for Doc, who was a bachelor. As new neighbors they carpooled to campus as often as they could.

The reference to Don Quixote in the poem "Turnabout" was a personal reminder of a running joke between them. Doc had teasingly referred to Bob as the incorrigible "Don Q," and

Bob, in turn, called Doc "Sancho." Shirley was his "female Sancho." He needed them both to help him make wise decisions as he fought his windmills and took on new challenges. "Turnabout," however, was not about Doc. It was, in part, autobiographical. Bob had developed a tendency toward enthusiastic elaboration, and at Gallaudet he quickly established a reputation among his students for running overtime during class sessions. He knew that he was known for his theatrical classroom style, but he apparently did not adhere to the Shakespearean proverb "Brevity is the soul of wit."

As Bob did his best to follow Doc's example and avoid fighting with the administration, he guided his students through the turmoil of changes in curriculum and academic requirements. He also began to work more and more in helping the students with the sign translations and coaching during the adaptations of plays. Among Bob's students was his former star pupil from Fanwood, Bernard Bragg. At Gallaudet, their friendship continued to grow, too. They attended off-campus college theater performances together, and into the late hours they would discuss acting, poetry, and other topics. As the writer Helen Powers later wrote, it was these discussions between student and teacher that formed the initial conception for a National Theatre of the Deaf:

> The word imagery and skillful expression that [Bragg] acquired writing poetry was an important link between his deafness and his acting. It was during these night-owl sessions with Panara that the two men began to dream wishfully of a theater for the deaf, as Bernard had made up his mind that this was how he wanted to make his living and spend his life.[6]

In 1953, Bob landed a ninety-six pound tuna while on a boat with his dad and several friends in Cape Cod Bay.

Bob's family was indeed proud of his becoming a college professor. Eleanor, too, was excelling. After completing her high school education, she had gone on to major in French at New Rochelle College for Women. She had graduated with honors in 1950 and had been teaching French at Somerset High School. She also married John Lynch, a Notre Dame alumnus whom she met on a cruise ship to Europe a few years earlier. He worked for the U.S. Tire and Rubber Company in Chicago. Bob and Shirley alternated their visits to their respective families in Missouri and Massachusetts. As business had picked up toward the end of the Depression, Bob's father bought a twenty-eight-foot cabin cruiser that he often used for deep-sea fishing. The elder Panara often gave the fish he caught to the nuns of the Convent of St. Thomas More in Somerset, which led him to be known as "St. John."

In October 1955, Shirley and Bob suffered a heartbreaking loss when their second child, David Robert, was stillborn. At Cheverly Hospital, Shirley nearly lost her life during this painful experience. For an entire week the family, including Bob, was not allowed to see her as she suffered labor pains. During the birth, Shirley's uterus ruptured, and she bled badly. Another specialist operated on her and saved her life. Bob did everything he could to avoid showing the grief and concern he was experiencing, especially when his brave wife apologized for losing the baby. There would be no more children.

Within a week after Shirley was brought home to their apartment in Kent Village, she developed a blood clot in her leg. It took months for her to recover, and Bob and Shirley were grateful for Shirley's mother, who came to help take care of young John while Bob returned to his teaching at Gallaudet.

Meanwhile, the oralism movement in the schools for deaf children continued to restrict many good deaf teachers to vocational education classes. Unable to teach speech, many bright deaf men and women were turned away from teaching at all.

Even at Gallaudet College the oral-versus-signing issue emerged on political and personal levels. Although Bob had become very proficient in sign language, he often mixed mime in with his instruction, and the fact that he sometimes used his voice in class bothered some deaf colleagues. This was a sensitive issue because in 1953 Dean Detmold had raised concerns among the faculty and students, as well as alumni, when he proposed a plan for compulsory oral training for all Gallaudet undergraduates.[7] Any use of speech by the deaf faculty might be interpreted as supporting Detmold's plan. In general, Bob was strongly opposed to oral instruction, and there had long been arguments against speaking and signing at the same time. In 1938, for example, Tom Anderson had summarized the arguments well in an article titled "What of the Sign Language?" Published in the *American Annals of the Deaf*, Anderson complained of the "mongrel gibberish" that often resulted when a person would try to address an assemblage simultaneously. "If the speaker's hands fall behind in the unequal race, the tongue wins."[8] Anderson also discussed how stress on English word order and thought alters the basic structure of the sign language. Even by 1938, the combined approach was "commonly attempted," but as Anderson bewailed, there were very few who could accomplish the task while maintaining the "grace and beauty of the [sign] language."[9]

There was also another reason for concern about Bob's teaching practices. Bob had learned how to mix sign and speech without losing clarity in his signs and crispness in his fingerspelling. It slowed the pace of his speaking somewhat, but this was not the problem. Rather, a couple of his deaf colleagues were afraid that his manner of teaching might lead others to believe that all deaf teachers could learn to speak as well. This perception would only complicate the politics that they were already facing in the profession.

At Gallaudet, the ratio of hearing to deaf faculty at the time Bob began teaching was two to one. Within a few years, Detmold's hiring of more Ph.D.'s changed that ratio to three to one. Little did the deaf faculty realize how many hearing

Ph.D.'s would come on board and leapfrog over them in rank and salary. Some of the deaf faculty had been there for fifteen or twenty years, but without a Ph.D., none had been promoted to full professorships. Several deaf faculty remained as chairs while others were replaced with new hires as Detmold continued to work toward accreditation and overhaul the Gallaudet curriculum and teaching requirements. Fortunately, the dean of instruction gave up the idea of compulsory oral education. However, in 1955, the same year he and Shirley lost their baby, Bob became one of Detmold's deaf victims. He was replaced as head of the English department by Dr. William Stokoe, a young hearing professor and a close friend of Detmold's. Stokoe had no prior exposure to educating deaf students, but he had earned a doctorate.

Bob was furious about this decision. While Detmold seemed to value his contributions, he did not seem to recognize the fact that Bob had been working toward his Ph.D. part-time at Catholic University. To make things worse, as Detmold added new courses to the curriculum, many of the new hearing teachers, including Stokoe, were unable to teach them. They could not sign well enough to effectively instruct deaf college students. As a result, Bob was assigned to teach Shakespeare, the Romantic period, the Victorian period, modern poetry, literary criticism, among other courses. In order to stay a step ahead of his classes, he took related courses at Catholic University.

During Stokoe's first year at Gallaudet, the deaf faculty treated him with civility. However, as he and Detmold became inseparable, their popularity quickly went downhill. They played tennis together daily and had their lunches off-campus, seldom mingling with the Gallaudet "regulars" and almost never dining in the college cafeteria. Stokoe was an expert on Chaucer, but after one year of instruction, it was clear to his colleagues that he lacked classroom teaching skills. As time went on, however, to Stokoe's credit he began making significant advances in researching the linguistics of sign language. He nevertheless remained rather awkward at using sign language. The prelingually deaf students at Gallaudet, who were more dependent on sign, simply could not fathom his attempts to teach Chaucer. Bob reflected on this years later: "It was rumored that Bill was getting students to read Chaucer aloud . . . if that really happened, there were only two people who knew—Bill Stokoe and God. And now, only God knows!"[10]

Ironically, one of Stokoe's first encounters with the effective use of sign language was in Bob Panara's classroom. He observed Bob discussing *Wuthering Heights,* shifting dramatic illustration from hand to hand as he referred to the characters Heathcliff and Cathy. As Stokoe later reflected, "It struck me at that time that here was an absolutely fascinating way of conducting a course in English literature, and it was something that I'd have to learn to do after some kind of fashion if I wanted to succeed in teaching my subject."[11]

Bob had taken over teaching Chaucer. Doc, who had never taught Chaucer before, was happy that the course was in good hands. Bob, however, was also expected to teach *Beowulf* and old English poetry as new courses for English majors. He was also ready to teach the humanities unit on Emerson, having studied that writer in depth at New York University. Bob had always admired Emerson's work, his poems, his essays, his transcendentalism, and, especially, his enthusiasm. Like his father, who had become so well-read that he had an almost religious admiration of the great minds that influenced him, Bob was especially inspired by reading Emerson, but also greatly influenced by John (Cardinal) Newman before his conversion from Anglicanism to Catholicism. Bob wrote several papers on Newman and was an advisor for the Newman Club at Gallaudet. The close affinity to nature of Wordsworth's earlier work also made an impression on him. Bob was a Unitarian, not necessarily in the formal sense, but certainly in the philosophical sense, though his beliefs sometimes bordered on the religious. He remained passionate over the works of the poet Shelley. Like Byron, he reasoned: "I love not man the less but nature more." With Shakespeare he reveled, "Under the greenwood tree, who loves to lie with me."

Indeed, "heart and soul" had become refrains in Bob's teaching. The 1951 Gallaudet yearbook, *The Tower Clock,* is peppered with Emerson's verse. There is no doubt where the students got their inspiration: Bob was faculty advisor. The quotes were some of his favorites, which apparently touched his students as well. "These are the voices / We hear in solitude." "Over everything stands it daemon, or soul, And, as the form of the thing is reflected by the eye, the soul of the thing is reflected by a melody." "My careful heart we free again,— / O friend, my bosom said, / Through thee alone the sky is arched, / Through thee the rose is red." And in 1955, the primary text for his humanities course was *The Complete Essays and Other Writings of Ralph Waldo Emerson.* In February that semester his course notes included an assignment in which he asked his students to examine how "inner revelation" was suggested in Emerson's poem "The Problem." In discussing the answer to this question, Bob wrote to his deaf students:

> Emerson stressed the divinity of nature, and, because of this divinity, he believed in the deep moral truths which emanated from its spiritual laws. By an alike analogy, he proclaimed the divinity of man as evidenced when the latter expresses his noblest ideals by way of intuition, of inspiration from the Universal Mind, or Over-Soul, or Deity.
>
> It is no use to preach to me from without. I can do that too easily myself. Jesus speaks always from within, and in a degree that transcends all others. In that is the miracle.[12]

The concept of "inner revelation" and Emerson's idea that "instinct is trust" can well explain how Bob Panara's own life shaped his teaching and won the hearts of his students.

The 1955–1956 school year ended on a tragic note, with the death of one of Bob's role models. It was early May, and the Gallaudet College students, who admired Frederick Hughes as much as Bob had when he was a student, had dedicated the yearbook with genuine affection to the sixty-four-year-old deaf professor of dramatics and economics. They, too, had recognized Hughes's contributions in scholarship, teaching, and sports. Deaf since the age of six, the graduate of the Gallaudet College class of 1913 had taught for more than forty years. "As long as strength of character and warmth of personality continue to inspire us," the yearbook stated, "his will be a lasting force and a guiding influence."

Touched as these words were read to him, Dr. Hughes accepted the yearbook on the stage in Chapel Hall. He thanked his students and colleagues and turned to go back to his seat next to his wife, Regina Olsen Hughes. Hughes took a few steps, suddenly stopped, and collapsed from a heart attack. He died shortly afterwards. Gone was the man who had worked so hard to cultivate the arts of acting and pantomime at the college where he had taught for more than forty years. He would especially be remembered for his productions of Gilbert and Sullivan, which he translated into sign language with a mastery that maintained the rhyme and rhythm in a magical way.

A few days later, Bob penned a tribute to his teacher and friend:

> The play is done, and now the curtain call
> Commands the youthful players to appear
> Upon their little stage so as to hear
> The tumult of applause in Chapel Hall
>
> Some marveled at the vivid fluency
> Of gestured woe and nimble-fingered joy;
> And others wondered at the strange alloy
> Of ragged bliss and kingly misery.
>
> And there, behind the scenes, still lingers on
> The Master's touch, who gave them to perceive
> That all this "sock and buskin" make-believe,
> Like some rehearsal for the life beyond,
> Puts Everyman on trial in the test
> To prove that he performed his very best.

In writing this poem about Frederick Hughes, Bob was developing a pattern in his personal verse that he had begun with the tribute to Percival Hall—using poetic "portraits" to honor great teachers who had touched his life in significant ways.

By 1957, Shirley had recovered, following a careful program of exercise. With a loan from his father, Bob made a down payment on a split-level home in Mustang Place in Riverdale, Maryland, into which they moved in February. Living in their first home was truly a joy, and the family grew to include Fritz, a German shepherd (and team mascot for John's baseball team), and Louie and Sandy, black and orange cats, all living in harmony. Bob and Shirley were often asked to be chaperones at college proms, picnics, and field trips. Living within short distances were close deaf friends such as Rex Lowman, Willard Madsen, Mac Norwood, and their families.

Bob also expanded his Deaf Studies work considerably by taking a major role in editing an anthology of works by deaf poets. Taras Denis, his former student, had collaborated with Bob in an earlier undertaking when they edited a volume of poetry by deaf writers. Begun in 1951, the first collection consisted of short stories, essays, and poems compiled from an accumulated literary stock at Gallaudet College, dating back to 1925. Some of the verse was written when the authors were college students. Other works were written while they were professionals. Work on *The Silent Muse: An Anthology of Prose and Poetry by the Deaf* began at the reunion of the Gallaudet College Alumni Association in 1957, when it was voted that urgent action be taken in sponsoring such a book. As the newly appointed editor-in-chief of the anthology, Bob began by revising the old manuscript in order to bring the project to fulfillment as quickly as possible. He also decided to include prose works, drawing from many short stories by deaf writers. With the assistance of Denis and John McFarlane, approximately 250 poems by deaf men and women were scrutinized, and this collection was narrowed down to a total of 100 poems, with 28 short stories.

"Poets are made as well as born," Bob wrote about *The Silent Muse* in the Gallaudet *Alumni Bulletin,* "and the inference here is that the deaf poet is ever improving, always learning, as his experiences with life and art take on newer and richer meanings, as his studies widen so as to include more models to imitate and new forms of expression by which to dress and clothe his art."[13] Whereas the first anthology had reflected the work of the "old school" of deaf poets in the main, those of the nineteenth century and the first quarter of the twentieth century, the new collection represented a more modern era in both prose and poetry. *The Silent Muse* spanned a period of 125 years, from 1835 to 1960, and included works from the better-known deaf authors, such as Laura Redden, Barry Miller, Howard L. Terry, George M. Teegarden, Joseph Schuyler Long, Alice McVan, Rex Lowman, Loy Golladay, Mervin Garretson, and Dorothy Miles. Bob wrote that this new anthology would "bring genuine surprise, and delight, and wonder to all those readers who appreciate the deaf writer's struggle to give artistic expression to the fire that burns within."[14]

Nineteen fifty-seven was also the year when Bob became part of the lore of the American deaf community. It began on the afternoon of October 15, when Gallaudet College president Leonard M. Elstad called Bob to his office and introduced him to the Washington, D.C., editor of *Life* magazine. As they explained to the deaf professor, Queen Elizabeth II was making her first visit to the United States, and while staying with President Eisenhower, she and Prince Philip were scheduled to watch the Maryland–North Carolina football game at the University of Maryland. Reporters were strictly forbidden from sitting anywhere near the queen or recording her comments. Undaunted, *Life* had an unusual request for young Bob, who had been recommended by Elstad. Would he be willing to "eavesdrop" by lipreading through a high-powered telescope? A reporter accompanying him would record the queen's comments, and those of her husband, Prince Philip, on a tape recorder. Bob was told that the operation was a "top secret" mission. He could only talk with Shirley and Dr. Elstad about the plans.

Bob's first reaction was that it was an impossible mission. Lipreading was no easy endeavor, he knew, but he was willing to give it a try. A few days before the game there was a "secret workout" to test their ability to lipread at a distance of two hundred yards.[15] It was the Wednesday before the game and the *Life* editor took Bob to the University of Maryland stadium, where two other *Life* reporters went up to sit across the field on the last row of seats as Bob watched through a telescope. As they talked about football, the weather, and other topics, Bob relayed their small talk to the *Life* editor. He got about 50 percent of the conversation, which sold the gig to the editor. Even so, during the discussion with the *Life* staff, he worried about the queen's British accent, so Bob recommended that a Gallaudet freshman, Alton Silvers, come along with him to the game as a backup lipreader. The telescope was also too heavy, and Bob joked that two eyes are better than one. The *Life* staff thus gave Bob a pair of binoculars. On game day at the stadium, Wilson H. Elkins, president of the University of Maryland, and Theodore McKeldin, the governor of Maryland, also were with the queen and the prince in the fifty-yard-line box seats. Continually lipreading while holding binoculars through the game proved to be exhausting. According to the resulting publication of *Life* magazine, however, the queen proved to be a "remarkably savvy spectator with a quick eye to pick out and a ready tongue to ask about the pertinent points of the game."[16] "Why are the goal posts behind the lines at the ends of the fields?" she asked, among other questions. Watching the huddle, she inquired, "Why do they gather that way?"[17] At one point she predicted a pass; at another time she expressed disappointment over a penalty on Maryland. There were many other questions, as well as some comments comparing American football to rugby in terms of the player "spills." The most frustrating thing about "Operation Lipread" for Bob was that "I had to keep my eyes glued to the Queen's face and couldn't watch the game!"[18] The teams were tied 7 to 7 at the halftime, and Maryland eventually won 21 to 7.

The magazine came out on October 28, six days after the game. Bob experienced various reactions to the *Life* article. He enjoyed reading the summary, although, because of confidentiality and secrecy, he was not mentioned by name in it. When he and Alton were later interviewed for the *Buff and Blue,* they were somewhat modest. Silvers said, "We were pretty lucky to be picked for the job—it was a thrill of a life time."[19] Bob added, complimenting *Life* for its skilled technical organization. "That's right—and we were just as fortunate that things turned out so well."[20] President Elstad at first congratulated them on showing the world that Gallaudet had good lipreaders, even though they had only captured about 40 percent of the queen's comments. However, a month later, Gallaudet Board members expressed concern about invading the queen's privacy, and Elstad made the decision not to support any similar stunts at secret lipreading that might come to the College. Shirley had her biggest laugh at the reaction of the board.

Bob would be the first to agree that there are many hazards associated with lipreading. One morning a short time after the *Life* magazine adventure, he was driving his son, John, and Mickey Garrison, a classmate, to school. Bob tried to strike up a conversation with the boy to put him at ease with regards to his deafness. First, he asked John what he wanted to be when he grew up, and John, well conditioned by his father, responded, "A baseball player!" "Good, wonderful," Bob said, and then he asked Mickey the same question. Looking away for a brief time from the road while driving, he saw the boy partly answer with, "A fireman." Again, he responded, "Good, wonderful!" The boys got out of the car with a rather uncomfortable look on their faces. Bob asked John that evening what had happened. Little Johnny answered, "Mickey said that he wanted to be a fireman, like his father, who died in a fire!" Deeply chagrined, Bob immediately got into his car and drove to the boy's house to apologize to him and his mother. "That's where deaf people put their foot in their mouths often," he said ruefully.[21]

Fiat Lux!

The contrast between Bob and the hearing Ph.D.'s being hired at Gallaudet was striking. Although Bob did not have a Ph.D., it was *his* class that visitors would flock to in order to see excellence in teaching. Colleagues stopped by to see why their students were so enthusiastic about Bob's style. Professors in the Normal Department brought their teacher candidates to observe him. President Elstad's wife also frequently brought groups to visit Bob's classes. Bob will never forget the night that the Panaras' next-door neighbor, Arnold Lau, dropped by for a visit. Arnie cocked his head and said, "Hi there, big shot!" Puzzled, Bob asked the Secret Service agent what he meant. Arnie explained that he was responsible for guarding President Eisenhower and that while he was in the office that day, Ike was meeting with Nelson Rockefeller, who was briefing him about his visit to Gallaudet College. Rockefeller, Ike's special advisor, was working for the Federal Security Agency's project to follow up on the Gallagher Report on higher educational opportunities for deaf people. As Arnie told Bob, Rockefeller suddenly began talking about what an exciting and illuminating experience he had while visiting the college. He spoke glowingly of observing a young professor who taught in both speech and sign language while discussing the poetry of Robert Frost.

Arnie apologized for the interruption and asked Rockefeller if he was talking about his neighbor, Robert Panara. Rockefeller immediately recognized the name given to him by the Gallaudet public relations director who had been his guide. He turned to President Eisenhower and commented that Arnie was indeed fortunate to have such a friend. Eisenhower, too, was interested in the story and commended Arnie for being so attentive and for having a deaf family as close friends.

In 1959, reporter Jim Mathis from the *Houston Post* visited the Gallaudet campus and provided a much more dramatic summary of Bob's teaching. As he wrote: "When the lecture began it was impressive and full of impact. On that particular day, Panara was explaining Emily Dickinson. Anyone could have learned more about Dickinson's brilliant choice of words on little things by listening for half an hour to Panara than in several full courses."[1]

Mathis described Bob's explanation of a loved one's death. "The sweeping up of the heart and putting love away / We shall not want to use again until eternity" was "visible and with movement of emotion." Bob's descriptions of a "narrow fellow in the grass," the famed snake, and "Zero in the Bone" were "precise and chilling." Although Mathis did not know signs, he saw the dramatic flair in Bob's interactions with his students. "And when he took Dickinson's train around the mountain it was with giant steps and with supercilious eyebrows at the shanties along the track as he choo-chooed along."[2]

Crisp signing, emphasized by a slightly slower pace and much drama was the way Bob taught. He would begin classes with something that caught the students' attention and that built their curiosity. One day, for example, he entered a dimly lit classroom and switched on the lights. He then wrote on the blackboard: "Fiat Lux!"—"Let there be light!" It was a great way to get his students started, and for teaching a little Latin as well. Indeed, his acting was entrancing.

Jack Gannon, who later became a highly respected author, best known for his books *Deaf Heritage* and *The Week the World Heard Gallaudet,* remembers Bob as his favorite teacher. "I'd sit down, get comfortable and he'd begin to take us deep into literature—and before I knew it, it was time to get up and leave! The information he shared and his delivery system—very theatrical—never ceased to keep me spellbound."[3] Bob had a profound influence on Gannon's love for writing. "I took an independent study course under him one year that involved a comparative study of great American writers, and that experience influenced my own writing style."[4] Over the next fifty years, Gannon would occasionally share his own pieces of writing with his former teacher. The mentorship became a friendship based on mutual appreciation for literature.

Patrick Graybill, who became a university professor and renowned actor in the National Theatre of the Deaf, also remembers his undergraduate years at Gallaudet under Bob's guidance. "I remember how brilliantly he narrated the classics like *Beowulf* and *Casey at the Bat.*" The translations into fluent and dynamic sign language were "like Houdini's incredible tricks."[5] "After meeting him, I knew I could depend on him for advice in the area of translating poems, stories, and plays as well as that of deciding which field to enter. He was one of the most skilled and sincere teachers in my life."[6] And Frances Parsons, another student of Bob's at Gallaudet who became a teacher and author of several books, including *Sound of the Stars* and *I Didn't Hear the Dragon Roar,* recalled Bob as "the most dynamic professor I ever met." As she explained, "Every time Robert entered the lecture room with his charming smile and twinkling eyes, he lit up the room. No student daydreamed or dozed off in his classes."[7] Fiat Lux!

Like Frances Parsons, Ray Parks Jr. modeled Bob's style when he entered teaching as a profession. Inspired by Bob as "one of the greatest educators," Parks cherished receiving the Robert F. Panara Deaf Education Award forty years later.[8]

When the Gallaudet Theatre was established to replace the annual plays of the Drama Club and those of the Kappa Gamma Fraternity, Bob helped to translate plays into sign language, including *Oedipus Rex, The Trojan Woman, Medea, Hamlet, Othello,* and *Romeo and Juliet.* Shortly after *Othello* was performed at Gallaudet in 1959, NBC contacted Gallaudet and asked if they could make a videotape of several scenes. The segment was shown nationally on the NBC network. As Bob's reputation spread, he continued to exert a motivating influence on his students, among them Eugene Bergman and Bernard Bragg, who both became masters of dramatic arts and literature themselves. Bergman became the first deaf person to earn a Ph.D. in English. He coedited *Angels and Outcasts,* an anthology of deaf characters in literature, and with Bragg, he authored several plays and books.

The life paths of Bernard Bragg and Bob crisscrossed many times after the Fanwood and Gallaudet years. The lasting impression Bob left with his student is best exemplified in Bragg's dedication of his book with Jack R. Olson, *Meeting Halfway in American Sign Language,* to his former teacher "who is, in the eyes of many, a shining model for clear communication in the Sign Language." In a copy he presented to Bob, Bragg inscribed: "As Hamlet says to his players, 'Speak the speech . . . trippingly on the tongue.' I know of no one who could sign more trippingly on the hands, face and body than my very first deaf teacher!" As Bob's student at Gallaudet, Bragg had become remarkable in his ability to interpret poetry via sign and in writing verse. In his senior year, Bob and Doc made up the committee that awarded the Teegarden Poetry Prize to Bragg. Bob was a proud teacher! And his students at Gallaudet were just as proud of Bob. Indeed, in 1961, *The Tower Clock,* Gallaudet's yearbook, was dedicated to Bob, who was honored for his "outstanding services as a teacher, advisor, and friend of the students of the college."[9]

In the course of editing the anthology *The Silent Muse,* Bob's interest in poetry, and particularly in the work of deaf poets, grew even further. Introduced at one convention banquet as an "authority on English poetry," he focused his presentation on the ability of deaf people, including those who were born deaf, to "write outstanding free verse."[10] He explained that those born deaf have little difficulty with metaphors but often struggle in writing metrical verse. Persons such as himself, who learned to read before becoming deaf, can often remember the rhythm of speech and poetry and have less difficulty with meter.

It was also Bob's sense of social acceptance in his elementary and secondary school years that planted the idea that deaf students did not necessarily have to be different in terms of their ability to understand and enjoy auditory-based verse. He was convinced that even with the obstacles they faced, the pleasure was theirs to discover. It only takes a good teacher to bring out an appreciation of language, both English and sign language.

Bob's work with the anthology also contained an element of empowerment. In 1961, the *British Deaf News* viewed *The Silent Muse* as a "political message." Besieged by oralism for too many years, the Deaf community in England was frustrated. The British journal staff saw this American publication as evidence of the good that could come out of "revitalizing" education through the natural medium of sign language:

> When the deaf in this country can read and write such verse as is contained in The Silent Muse then the battle will be won and there will be no need to talk of "integration." . . . The Silent Muse shows what might be achieved if prejudice were set aside and the proper needs of the deaf considered. The great needs of deaf children in this country today are the greater educational opportunities of time and method. When these are forthcoming we may envisage . . . a more literate deaf population.[11]

Bob continued to pursue his interest in poetry the following year, 1962, when he addressed a group of English teachers at a conference in Washington, D.C. He explained that while many deaf college students struggle with self-expression and its relation to the writer's point of view, in the case of poetry, because of its use of compressed meaning and figurative language, poetry is something of an enigma.[12] Bob argued that many teachers don't realize that words are of less importance than ideas. "A treasury of words," he emphasized, "is of little value unless the student knows how to use them."[13]

Bob was also in tune with a wide range of hearing writers. He interacted with some of them during the Ballard Literary Society meetings. One evening, Leo Brady, author of the novel *The Edge of Doom* and the Broadway play *Yankee Doodle,* came to talk with the students. Bob and the students had finished a program of poetry and short stories in sign language, and Bob introduced Brady, extolling his work. Brady walked onto the stage and began with some opening remarks that were meant to be humorous, but in their delivery they became potent as an agent for change for the Literary Society's focus. He glanced over at Assistant Dean Elizabeth Benson, who was interpreting, and then looked at the group of students in Chapel Hall. "I was impressed with how you interpreted those poems and short stories in sign, and Professor Panara tells me that is one of the main functions of your Literary Society. However, it seems to me that the true purpose and function of a Literary Society or Circle is to Create and Write!"[14]

Brady then admonished the students with a witty grin: "Why are you all sitting here, when you should be at your desk in the dormitory pushing a pen or hitting the keys of your typewriters?"[15] He explained that when he was a student, that was what the Literary Circle at Catholic University did, and he added wryly, "Today, the students in our Literary Society are doing much the same as you . . . although without your skill and expressiveness in dramatic sign language!"[16] Brady's observations were not ignored. After his visit, Bob held discussions with the students. "Not long after," he reflected, "we started to include those poems and short stories that were actually created and written by the students at Gallaudet."[17]

By now, Bob also had his successful former student, Bernard Bragg, the "Master of Mime," to hold up as a model storyteller. Working for San Francisco's educational television station KQED in 1962 as "The Quiet Man," Bragg was capturing the imagination of thousands of children through his entertaining stories and pantomime. "Friendships such as ours," Bragg wrote to Bob that year, "are the real thing that makes life our grand world."[18]

Shirley, of course, supported Bob in all of his endeavors and shared his friendships with former and current students and colleagues. She was one of the first deaf people to hold a position as a cataloguer at the Library of Congress. She did so well at the American Meteorological Society that she advanced from cataloguer to indexer and then technical writer to summarize as abstracts various meteorological reports in English. For eight years, she honed her skills in library science, focusing her reading time on the subject of meteorology, abstract writing, and bibliographies. This soon came in handy when she began to work with Bob to write captions for movie scripts for the U.S. government's Captioned Film Bureau. Shirley insisted on keeping her almost full-time position with the Library of Congress, however. She wanted to be home by 3:30 p.m. every day when young Johnny arrived from school.

John was now old enough to join Bob on the summer fishing excursions on his grandfather's boat. At the age of eight, he had landed two fish on his first try. Bob and Shirley had him catching baseballs when he was four years old. At the age of ten, he was playing for the St. Bernard's B Midget Team in the Catholic Youth Organization (CYO). Bob was the coach and Shirley was the scorekeeper for almost six years. His experiences in managing that team in the Greater Washington, D.C., CYO

St. Bernard's Little League baseball team. Coach Bob Panara (front center) and son John (third from right) helped take the team to the CYO finals three straight years.

League, in which John pitched and played first base, were among Bob's fondest memories of his son's childhood. That is, except for the three straight times the team played in the CYO championship game—and lost!

At this point Bob experienced a turning point in his life as a baseball fan. John's dragging him to Griffith Stadium to see his heroes—sluggers Roy Sievers, Bob Allison, Harmon Killebrew, and other players—led Bob to finally change team colors. He now had a new "home team," but this lasted only a few years. The Washington Senators' move to Minnesota left the Panara family disappointed.

John knew well how much his dad enjoyed learning the words to new hit songs. When he was little, he used to transcribe tunes for his dad on an RCA record player. The boy often had to replace its needle because of the difficulty in handling the arm of the record player when he was transcribing. While spinning a record, he would catch a lyric, pick up the arm *(scraaatch!)*, write down the song line, place the arm back down on the record *(scraaatch!)*, listen to more lyrics, lift up the arm again, write down another line, then drop the arm *(scraaatch!)*. As John reminisced:

> Of all those transcribed songs, the one that gave my father the most pleasure in learning and then singing was "You Gotta Have Heart." It comes from the soundtrack to *Damn Yankees*, the Broadway play that became a movie about a guy who sells his soul to the devil in order to become a star on the Washington Senators and lead his team over the Bronx Bombers. The song is fairly long and took a while for me to transcribe, but it was worth it for two reasons. First, my father got a great kick out of singing those lyrics. For a while, every Saturday morning I'd awaken to Dad belting out, "You Gotta Have Heart." Second, before that tune came along, my father had sung Irving Berlin's, "Oh, How I Hate to Get Up in the Morning" on most Saturdays. I was getting kind of sick of that song. "You Gotta Have Heart" was a good replacement![19]

By 1963, Bob had more or less perfected his teaching style with its emphasis on dramatization. His real goal was to focus on reaching every student in the classroom. Ever since his first teaching assignments at Fanwood, he recognized that any given classroom would probably contain a wide range of deaf students. Some might be fluent signers, while others knew only a little. Some used hearing aids, while others did not. Some could read lips, while their peers had no such ability. Bob focused on finding his own style in the classroom, and he encouraged his colleagues to find theirs. No one philosophy or technique worked perfectly for all teachers. Bob had already seen how his style was shaped by his former teachers. He helped his colleagues discover how each of them could find the strategies that worked best.

Apparently in 1963 word had gotten out about how his style was endearing his students to learning. That year, he was invited to present a teaching demonstration at the International Congress on the Education of the Deaf (ICED). Lloyd Ambrosen, the superintendent at the Maryland School for the Deaf, was the program chair and Bob agreed to present two sessions on poetry, each one and a half hours long. At the time, Gallaudet College had only one building with air conditioning: the new Elstad Auditorium, seating eight hundred people.

Bob's challenging teaching demonstration focused on the work of such writers as Emily Dickinson, Robert Frost, and e. e. cummings. With this representative group of ten deaf students from the junior and senior classes of Gallaudet College, Bob used all forms of communication, including fingerspelling, sign language, pantomime, and the printed word. People flocked to him after the session was over. Among them was Margery Hall, President Percival Hall's daughter-in-law, who wrote him a personal note, "I've had the e. e. cummings pages on my desk ever since that . . . afternoon at the Congress when I heard your classroom lecture on his poetry. . . . How privileged your students are to study under you!"[20]

A press release from ICED came out on August 1, 1963. Dr. M. J. C. Buchli of Groningen, the Netherlands, and past president of the International Congress, reported that in the "Response for Foreign Delegates" at the Banquet, they had named one of the two high points of the Congress the "Class in American Literature" demonstration by a deaf professor, Robert F. Panara. It also marked the first time in the ICED's long history a deaf teacher had ever presented at its convention.

Meanwhile, Bill Stokoe continued to lay the theoretical foundations for American Sign Language (ASL) to be eventually recognized as a language. Like many other faculty at Gallaudet, Bob was not closely following this work. He and Stokoe were "friendly colleagues," who would have been closer had Dean Detmold not aligned himself with the linguist. When Stokoe published his now classic seminal studies, especially *Sign Language Structure,* the summaries of his research simply remained incomprehensible to many in the profession. Most of his colleagues did not know anything about the linguistics of sign language, and some wondered why he was dissecting a language he couldn't even handle himself.

Bob had finished most of his doctoral studies several years earlier, including such requirements as literary criticism and prosody, and others in English literature, with a concentration on the Romantic period, the Victorian period, Shakespeare, and Chaucer. He had decided to do something original with his dissertation, focusing on "Deaf Characters in Fiction and Drama." Edward Cain, chairman of the English Department at Catholic University, warned him that he would have difficulty finding faculty qualified to advise him on that subject. Bob remained adamant, and Cain accepted the role of advisor.

In 1965, after Bob passed the two full-day comprehensive exams of five hours each, Cain began reading novels, short stories, and plays containing deaf characters. Then, one day about two months later, Bob received word at Gallaudet, through a phone call from Catholic University, that Cain had died suddenly of a heart attack.

With a Ph.D. all but in his hand and a sterling record as a teacher, he went to see Detmold. Bob had an international reputation and had distinguished himself in many ways that outshined the performance of most of his colleagues, many whom did not have Ph.D.'s. He was close to getting one. It would prove to be a pivotal meeting, although not for the reasons Bob had hoped.

Detmold knew well what a good teacher Bob was and what he had done and what he could do for him in theater. In the meeting Bob demanded pay equal to a full professor, even though he was still an associate professor. Detmold looked at Bob for a long moment. He said he valued Bob at Gallaudet, but he had to follow the policies in the faculty handbook. The dean's refusal to give him a raise was definitive. Right or wrong about the salary issue, Bob knew that it was the last time he and Detmold would ever sit down together. The experience convinced him of one thing—he was ready for a change.

Mending Wall

Change was indeed on Bob's horizon. In early November 1965, he received a letter from John Gardner, U.S. secretary of education, inviting him to serve on a National Advisory Board for the establishment of the National Technical Institute for the Deaf (NTID), a new college being planned with an emphasis on technical and vocational education for deaf students. Secretary Gardner explained that the group being formed was composed of national leaders in the education of the deaf and in the fields of administration, higher education, industry, and public affairs. Public Law 89-36 had authorized that board to facilitate the establishment, construction, and operation of a postsecondary facility for the technical training and education of deaf persons, and Gardner indicated in his letter that the effectiveness of the entire project would depend on the "advice and counsel" of the "best minds and talent" that could be found.[1] In the invitation, Gardner suggested that Bob's experience and judgment would be "extremely valuable to the work of the Board."[2]

Such a college was a dream long held in the Deaf community. For more than a century, deaf people had been calling for more opportunities to pursue technical education.[3] Since 1864, Gallaudet College had served as an established tradition of excellence in the field of liberal arts, but this was not enough to satisfy the Deaf community in America. As a faculty member at Gallaudet, Bob had little time to think about whether to accept this position. The idea of contributing to the establishment of this new college—one that integrated deaf and hearing students—was enticing, but he sensed mixed emotions among his deaf and hearing friends who were loyal to Gallaudet. Undaunted, within a few days he responded to Gardner that he would serve.

Progress made by the advisory board was swift. The first two-day session in Washington, D.C., took place within a month after Bob received Gardner's letter. The second meeting was convened in Los Angeles, California, the following month. By February 1966, a conference had been held in Chicago, with thirty-two representatives from twenty-four colleges and universities, all interested in sponsoring NTID. At the conference, the representatives were educated about the significant challenges that they would encounter in effecting a transition from their institutions' current populations of hearing students to a "changing clientele" that included a substantial number of deaf students.

Bob Panara's role on the board was as an experienced educator of deaf students at both high school and college levels. He had a profound impact on the discussions, drawing from his personal experiences to help the other members understand the impact of deafness on learning. Despite the progress, strong and diverse attitudes nearly aborted the NTID project during the early months of the National Advisory Board's work. The pessimism found in a national commission document, known as the Babbidge Report, in particular, planted doubts in the minds of a number of board members about the success experienced to date by educators of deaf students. One concern focused on the purpose of NTID. Some educators in schools serving deaf students stressed the need for "vocational" education. Baird, who came from a technical facility, spent considerable time clarifying the difference between "technical" and "industrial" education to the board. Other members of the deaf community believed that NTID should focus primarily on fulfilling the needs of the hundreds of students who could not meet the Gallaudet entrance examination requirements or who were unable to remain at Gallaudet until graduation. It was finally made clear that NTID was *not* to become a fallback trade school for deaf students. The meetings of the board were open to the public, and representatives of the Deaf community attended, including such prominent people as Frederick C. Schreiber of the National Association of the Deaf (NAD), Frank Sullivan from the National Fraternal Society of the Deaf, and Robert Sanderson, who represented Vocational Rehabilitation of Utah.

Wherever he went, Bob often felt the heat during behind-the-scenes discussions with other deaf people. During one evening with Deaf community members at a captioned film showing and potluck dinner at Mac Norwood's house, Fred Schreiber, Alex Fleischmann, and a few other deaf leaders cornered Bob and began harassing him as to what was going on. They wanted to know why there weren't more deaf people on the board. Of particular concern was the lack of members from NAD, which had a long and distinguished history of advocacy and empowerment for deaf people. The Deaf community leaders were also angry that NAD wasn't getting enough information from the board about the progress of its work.

Bob had added quite a few gray hairs to his head. He later wrote to Ralph Hoag, the project director of the National Advisory Board and later the superintendent of the Rochester School for the Deaf when NTID was established, "I had to do all I could to stay on an even keel and remain objective and 'cool' in all those interface situations at Faculty meetings and with the Student Body—let alone class sessions!"[4]

On January 11, 1967, shortly after the Rochester Institute of Technology (RIT) was selected as the host institution for the new National Technical Institute for the Deaf, RIT president Mark Ellingson and Arthur L. Stern, chairman of the RIT Board of Trustees, invited D. Robert Frisina, then a hearing dean of the graduate school at Gallaudet College, to be the founding director of NTID and vice president of RIT.

In the spring 1967, Bob Panara became the first person Frisina hired for NTID's faculty. They had been friends and colleagues at Gallaudet College. Frisina reflected later, "What better way to introduce RIT staff and students than a model capable of teaching both deaf and hearing students!"[5] Despite his loyalty to his employer and his alma mater, Bob knew that the Deaf community had long sought expanded opportunities in areas of study that Gallaudet was not able to offer. Even as far back as the nineteenth century there had been debate over establishing a national technical school for the deaf.[6] Unlike some in the Deaf community, Bob didn't see the creation of another college as competition with Gallaudet. Rather, he perceived it as the opportunity of a lifetime. In leaving Gallaudet for his new adventure, Bob thought of the words of Robert Frost in "Mending Wall": "Something there is that doesn't love a wall, that wants it down." He saw the challenge of building the new college as one of tearing down a wall that separated deaf and hearing people. Having benefited from an education in both mainstream and residential environments, he felt well prepared to tear down the walls.

Doc fully understood Bob's feelings about the new opportunity. Stokoe also wished him well, and having grown up in Rochester, he advised Bob that the town of Henrietta, which Bob had expressed an interest in, was a nice place to live. Many of Bob's other friends were busy with the upcoming graduation ceremonies, but they were not surprised about his decision to resign from the faculty. Bob left Gallaudet with many fond memories and a sense of gratitude. The college had been *his* stepping-stone to a successful career. While he was packing his bags and getting ready for his new adventure, he sat down and wrote a touching poem to his alma mater, titled "Hail and Farewell."

As if setting up a new college for deaf students was not enough, another opportunity was pulling Bob in a different direction that summer. Earlier, he had met David Hays at Gallaudet after a performance of *Our Town*. Hays, a noted Broadway figure, had been the set designer for *The Miracle Worker*, and encouraged by others, he developed an interest in forming a repertory group, a professional theater for deaf people that would showcase their unique brand of expression through sign and sign-mime. So while the Panaras were preparing for the move to Rochester, Hays invited Bob and about twenty-five other deaf people with experience in college and community theater to the first "Summer School" program for the National Theatre of the Deaf at the Eugene O'Neill Memorial Theatre Foundation in Waterford, Connecticut. Many of his close friends would be there, including Bernard Bragg and Eric Malzkuhn. The first plays were chosen for the tour, along with the cast and staff who would translate the plays. Hays remembered that Bob was "one of the people who called in right off the bat from the deaf community to advise us. He helped us to identify all the fine deaf actors he knew of in the deaf community."[7]

Shirley knew that this was another dream of Bob's that he couldn't refuse, but the timing was bad. She nevertheless supported him and offered to accept the formidable task of packing up the house alone for the move to Rochester.

Bob roomed with Malz, and they translated Puccini's operetta, *Gianni Schicchi,* a romantic farce, into sign language. Then Bob worked with Sahomi Tachibana, an expert in Kabuki drama, to translate *The Tale of Kasane.* Those two works, along with *The Man with his Heart in the Highlands* and *Tyger! Tyger! And Other Burnings,* were presented on the group's first national tour. The spacious lawns and beautiful landscapes of Waterford were idyllic. The Eugene O'Neill Memorial Theatre Center served as the NTD's home base. There was an old red barn remodeled to house the large laboratory theater and classrooms, and an old sprawling mansion with a dozen rooms to house students and faculty. Bob and his fellow consultants, Bernard Bragg and Malz, called it the Summer School by the Sea, as it was near the Long Island Sound just across from the Hamptons. Whenever he had the chance, Bob went to the sound to swim, bringing back memories of his high school and college years.

Bob spent a month with NTD, leaving Shirley in Maryland. Their home had been sold, and the move to Rochester was set for August 30. Bob was supposed to leave Waterford on August 20, but bad weather grounded all commuter planes to La Guardia. With his old colleague from Fanwood, Lou Fant, interpreting, Bob called his son, John, to let Shirley know. All John could tell his father was that "Mom was hopping mad." Bob tried to reach Shirley several more times but got the same dreaded message. When he finally arrived home on August 23, Shirley and John met him at the airport. Shirley's face was frozen. "Her steely blue eyes literally bored holes into mine." Hardly a word was exchanged on the drive home and for the next two days while packing boxes.[8] The excitement of the move, however, finally broke the ice and Bob, Shirley, and John left Maryland with their pets for a "great adventure."

Field of Dreams

The cinema hit *Field of Dreams* is a fascinating baseball story, an adaptation of W. P. Kinsella's novel *Shoeless Joe,* about a mystical cornfield in Iowa that is transformed into a baseball field where the likes of Shoeless Joe Jackson, his teammates from the infamous 1919 Chicago Black Sox scandal, and other baseball outcasts are resurrected to play another game. The movie is also about the power of dreams. "If you build it, they will come" are the magical words in this movie, a nice baseball metaphor for Bob's arrival in Rochester, New York, in 1967. That was no magical transformation of the marshlands of the Rochester Institute of Technology's campus and the building of the facilities for a technical college for deaf students. Rather, the message Bob sensed as he began this new adventure was that he could pursue all sorts of new dreams by coming to RIT. A college for deaf students in a mainstream environment truly excited him. It had never been done before. He had the confidence that he could break new ground in teaching deaf students and that, if he helped Bob Frisina plan this new college well, they *would* come.

Field of Dreams is also a story about ghosts; Bob had his own set of ghosts as he helped to build NTID. One ghost was renowned in the world of Deaf education—Laurent Clerc—the first deaf teacher in America. Clerc had paved a new path, working alongside Thomas Hopkins Gallaudet in founding the first state-sponsored school for deaf children in Hartford in 1817, the American School for the Deaf, where Bob experienced his first immersion in the Deaf community. There he taught other professionals sign language and how to educate deaf students. In wooing Bob to relocate to Rochester, Frisina indicated that the deaf professor would be the "Laurent Clerc of this new college."[1] Bob would be the first deaf teacher employed within a mainstream postsecondary program with a substantial number of deaf students. Like Clerc, he would also teach sign language and methods of instructing large numbers of deaf students. However, Bob's challenge, unlike Clerc's, was on the college level.

Bob's second ghost was from the world of baseball—that of Jackie Robinson. When Bob first accepted the invitation from Secretary Gardner to serve on the NTID Advisory Board, he met with some resistance from deaf friends who questioned why the new college had to be affiliated with an institution that also served hearing students. In his assimilation into RIT as a mainstream university, he faced a variety of attitudes among faculty and students who were not ready to accept the differences they saw in deaf learners—in particular, the unique cultural and communicative characteristics of this group of students. Many wondered how a small minority of deaf students could be integrated with the thousands of hearing students at RIT. It had never been done before on this level.

The "doubting Thomases" who predicted a short life span for NTID included parents, teacher organizations, rehabilitation counselors, and other national groups. "Ironically," Bob reflected, "many of these teachers were graduates of Gallaudet . . . like myself, and time and again, while . . . giving slide lectures about NTID, I had to try and convince them that Rome was not built in one day, and why 'the impossible dream' was slowly but surely taking on a way, shape, and form."[2]

Whereas Jackie Robinson, in his much more difficult experience as an African American baseball player, had broken down the racial barrier in professional baseball, Bob had to help dismantle the communication barrier between hearing and deaf people on the RIT campus.

When Bob arrived at NTID in 1967, there were several hundred students enrolled at Gallaudet College and no more than a total of 150 deaf students attending all other colleges and universities in the United States combined, most with no support services such as interpreting, notetaking, or tutoring. President Lyndon Baines Johnson's signing of the NTID bill on June 8, 1965, was about the power of dreams. The establishment of a mecca in technical education for deaf students was soon followed by the creation of other similar programs around the country. Within forty years there would be more than thirty thousand deaf and hard-of-hearing students in American postsecondary institutions.

Bob had also found a way to bring his new adventure in theater to Rochester, at least for a weekend, when he helped to plan NTD's debut at the new Nazareth Arts Center for

September 30, 1967. He and Eric Malzkuhn had adapted *Gianni Schicchi*, one of the four plays in the Rochester debut. Bob also worked with Sahomi Tachibana to adapt *The Tale of Kasane*. Third, one of the four signed poems was Bob's "On His Deafness." Jack Gould of the *New York Times* reviewed the NTD as "both a moving and exciting experience. . . . Moving because it illustrated how much beautiful expressiveness can be conveyed in the language of the hands and exciting because it opened up horizons on how much more may be done with a neglected branch of theatrical art."[3]

Frisina was delighted with the exposure that the National Theatre of the Deaf brought to the talents of deaf people as the new college began to operate. He viewed the National Technical Institute for the Deaf as an "experiment to determine whether deaf students, when provided appropriate education, could earn parity in the economic mainstream."[4] But the "Grand Experiment," as he called it, was made much harder to accomplish by the fact that there were no models. NTID would have to *become* the model. But this could not happen without Bob giving up teaching for a while to take on many different roles. He was, in effect, a utility man playing several positions. In preparation for the "charter class," the first group of deaf students, who would arrive in the fall of 1968, he met with every RIT student organization. He provided hearing students, as well as the faculty and staff, with some background and understanding as to the significance of this new college for deaf students. In October 1967 he helped to lead a two-day workshop for representatives of RIT student personnel. The focus was on counseling deaf students.

Since its inception in 1847, the Rochester Institute of Technology's "industrial education" programs had attracted deaf students. When Bob arrived in 1967, there were eight deaf students enrolled. In February 1968 Bob had a dinner meeting with seven of them. Three were profoundly deaf, two were severely hard-of-hearing, and two had slight hearing losses. The purpose of the meeting was to identify the barriers they had faced during actual classroom and lab experiences. These were the real Jackie Robinsons in this game, and Bob hoped that their sharing of their experiences would help level the playing field at RIT. The students were having difficulty in understanding the content of lectures delivered orally in class. The technical subject matter and "shop language" made lipreading virtually impossible. Instructors often turned their backs to them, and these students had to rely heavily on notes taken by hearing peers. These comments brought back memories of Bob's days at Clinton High.

In 1968, there were no trained interpreters yet at RIT. Nor was technology of much assistance. One deaf RIT student had tried using a tape recorder, but he found this approach ineffective. His wife interpreted the tape in sign language at home, but this method required five to seven hours to cover the content of a two-hour class. To make it even more difficult, his wife was unfamiliar with the subject. Another student had secured some tutoring from a hearing senior at RIT who was majoring in mathematics and who was familiar with sign language. Several students had asked peers to help with notes. In recommending the that interpreters, tutors, and note takers be made available for RIT classes, Bob put himself in the position of having to help prepare the support staff for the students about to enter NTID.

There was much work to be done in preparation for the arrival of the charter class, including the development of educational program requirements, the hiring of professional personnel, and the implementation of training programs to prepare RIT staff and students. Frisina hired E. Ross Stuckless for research and development, and Bill Williams to assist with financial planning. Along with other faculty and staff hired over the next year, Bob continued helping with public relations. During one national conference at New Mexico State University, Las Cruces, Bob and Ross Stuckless promoted NTID in their exchanges with other educators of deaf students. The conference went well, and on the last day, they had to find a ride from their motel to a chartered bus two miles away. One of Bob's former Gallaudet classmates, who had promised to take them to the bus, did not show up on time, and after waiting for fifteen minutes, Bob and Ross hailed a cab. In broken Spanish, Ross told the cab driver, "Drive like crazy and catch up with the already departed bus." After going about six miles at seventy-five miles per hour, they caught up with the bus, flagged it down, and joined their colleagues for the fifty-mile ride to the airport. "We had to grin and bear it while our colleagues gave us the 'raspberries' all the way to El Paso. We got them to admit, however, that it was the perfect 'PR stunt' for drawing attention to NTID and its 'innovative mission.'"[5]

On April 1, 1968, Frisina hired William E. Castle to assist him in the administration of the academic programs. Castle was then serving as associate secretary for research and scientific affairs for the American Speech and Hearing Association and had been on the faculty at State College in St. Cloud, Minnesota, Central Washington State College, and the University of Virginia. Frisina felt Castle was an excellent choice on several levels—particularly his research, clinical, and teaching background in communication; his work in professional organizations serving deaf people; his knowledge of government agencies and funding; and his interest and experience in higher education.

That spring, Bob helped Frisina and Castle present an evening series focusing on an orientation to deafness and the "Grand Experiment." Participants included 57 community representatives from business, industry, education, and the general public. The following summer, about 50 RIT faculty members received special training to prepare themselves for teaching the charter class of deaf students. The program emphasized communication, the visual presentation of information, and the impact of deafness on learning. In addition, more than 125 hearing students at RIT accepted Bob's invitation to learn sign language.

Bob understood that he was needed to help start up the college, but his real reason for coming to NTID was to teach. Setting up the college had been a process of improvisation from the start, and Bob could not wait to begin teaching again—this time in integrated classes. It was the education of students, not the formulation of organizational charts, that would make this college great. Yet it would be another year—with the charter class—before he could stand in front of a classroom again and teach his beloved humanities. Bill Castle was also an enthusiastic advocate of the value of the arts, especially literature and theater, in a technical college environment. From the start, he supported Bob's work in making literature and the performing arts an integral component of the NTID curriculum and a signature program that brought visibility to the college locally, nationally, and internationally. Bob could not have asked for a better dean during these early years.

As described earlier, the field of Deaf education has long been immersed in a bitter debate between those who believed that deaf students should be educated primarily through sign language and those who promoted oralism, the strict emphasis on the use of speech, residual hearing, and speechreading. The latter group is usually against the use of sign language in any form. While there have always been proponents on both ends of the spectrum, many deaf and hearing persons have found themselves somewhere in between. Some find it difficult to speak and sign at the same time. Speaking can interfere with the clarity of the signing. Certain deaf people who do not use speech might sign and shape their lips with the words. Others only sign. Students and professionals are always adjusting to individual preferences, and there has never been any research that convincingly supported the effectiveness of one modality of communication over another in terms of its impact on learning. But in light of the fact that classes are often heterogeneous mixes of students with a range of sign skills and residual hearing, the primary concern for good teachers has been the goal of reaching each and every deaf student in the classroom.

Bob never felt that he had to choose between ASL and English. He accepted each on its own terms and adapted to every situation as best he could when he taught his classes using sign language. Yet, as time passed, he began to see some of his colleagues at Gallaudet, NTID, and in other programs, develop factions advocating ASL or modes of signing in English word order. In nearly every class Bob taught, he encountered a range of communication skills and preferences. Now at NTID, he more or less found himself responsible for helping other new teachers in the field become familiar with best approaches. This was not easy in this sometimes politically charged environment. Bob recognized that other teachers would have to discover for themselves the best way to use sign language. He had developed his teaching style during a period when sign language was being transformed into a form of visual expression, one that, as he quoted from Shakespeare's *Hamlet,* "suits the action to the word."[6] In the years before the National Theatre of the Deaf helped increase the exposure of the general public to the beauty of signs through mass media, sign language was more "like the ugly duckling."[7] Rather than creating a sense of curiosity and attraction, he remembered how signing in public actually generated ridicule among some hearing people—there was a general perception of sign language as a "primitive" form of communication.

In a fact that many found ironic, William Stokoe had a lot to do with changing that. ASL slowly came to be recognized as a legitimate language. The publication in 1965 of *A Dictionary of American Sign Language on Linguistic Principles* by William Stokoe, with two deaf colleagues, Dorothy Casterline and Carl Croneberg, helped attract the attention of noted linguists, but that work had come out only a few years earlier.[8] As Bob explained, "We began to realize that Stokoe *did* succeed at a pioneering work, making a scientific and descriptive study of our language of signs."[9]

There was also a movement that ran counter to the emphasis on ASL. It was the philosophy of "Total Communication," which encompassed ASL, Signed English, fingerspelling, speech, and other elements used by teachers to address the diverse needs of students in the classroom; it had also become an emergent movement in Deaf education. During NTID staff meetings, discussions of these differing approaches occasionally escalated into heated disagreement. More than once during an emotional debate Bob would challenge comments made by colleagues and administrators. He saw the value and beauty of ASL, but he argued against those who advocated the use of that language as the sole means of communication in the classroom. Bob's belief was that the beauty of both English and ASL *could* be enjoyed in unison. He had seen its success in one of his role models, Powrie Vaux Doctor, at Gallaudet College. But he also sought to emulate the beauty of Frederick Hughes's signing—without voice—when such opportunities arose to communicate the abstraction in a purely visual way. This was ASL's place in Bob's teaching—a valuable tool, but only *one* of many in his teaching toolbox. He frequently emphasized the rightful place of ASL in teaching. Together, English and ASL became essential elements in his instructional approach.

In one of his first professional presentations as an NTID faculty member, in 1968, Bob provided a rationale for his approach to teaching. At the inaugural conference of the Council of Organizations Serving the Deaf, he cited Marshall McLuhan's *The Medium Is the Message*. "The method of our times," he told the audience of educators, "is to use not a single but multiple models for exploration" relative to the act of effective communication.[10] Bob argued that communication with deaf students often fails to produce the desired results because too much emphasis has been placed on only one method of communication. While it has taken centuries for educators to explore each of the methods used today in the schools and classes for deaf students, including the oral method, fingerspelling, and sign language, he explained, the paradox is that they had yet to make a concerted effort to address the needs of all students, "especially in schoolrooms and situations where the deaf are mismatched because of wide differences in their background—physical, educational, social, cultural." Bob reflected further on the value of signing: "In order to communicate effectively, and fluently, *people must feel at home in their language,* and the deaf are no exception."[11]

That June, Bob presented a paper titled "Poetry as a Language Learning Tool for Deaf Persons" at the International Research Seminar on the Vocational Rehabilitation of Deaf Persons. In this paper, Bob further elaborated on his integrative teaching style. Poetry, he explained, is "written in the faith that there would always be people who were capable of reproducing its imagery, its rhythm, and its eloquence." He went on to describe how the ancient Greeks called them "rhapsodes" and how that tradition has extended to today's classrooms. "What good would all these poems be," Bob asked, "if the world had no such rhapsodes and teachers?"[12]

In September 1968, NTID's "charter class," a specially selected group of young deaf men and women, arrived at RIT.
They were supposed to pursue bachelor degree studies while the
new faculty and staff hired by Frisina and Castle would continue to develop the diploma, associate, and general preparatory programs for deaf students who would enter in subsequent
years. Great care had been taken to ensure that the students
chosen for this program were capable, mature, and aware of the
responsibility they had to set the pace for future classes. The
main purpose of enrolling the charter class in 1968 was to give
RIT faculty and staff some experience with deaf students, and
to allow NTID the opportunity to determine what types of
programming would be necessary and how to phase in specialized support services. It was a timely experiment. RIT was just
beginning a new era as a major residential institute of technology. Frisina compared the charter students to "fish in a fish-
bowl," telling them that the eyes of the nation were on them.
They were being studied carefully to see how they could succeed on a campus of a hearing college, something never before
attempted with such a large number of students.

What followed was disappointing, however. It didn't matter that the charter class students had been carefully selected
and that the staff enthusiastically supported them. The "Grand
Experiment" had included too many variables. Time would be
needed to find the most effective strategies. Bob was reminded
of his own experience when he first thought about college. As
he had been in his younger years, some of the charter class students were unfamiliar with living and studying with other deaf
students, most of whom used sign language. Unlike Bob, most
of the charter students were inadequately prepared for the rig-

ors of the RIT curriculum. Learning through support services such as notetaking, interpreting, and tutoring was also an untested approach. As the year progressed, it became clear that a special program would be needed to provide incoming deaf students with more preparation before making the transition to the mainstream classes with hearing peers. Thus, as the first year came to an end, Bob was assigned the additional responsibility of developing the curriculum for the English Department in NTID's new "Vestibule Program."

As was his habit, whenever Bob needed some time alone to think about his life, he would find a "Walden Pond." In Rochester, he began his long walks near his home, taking in the smell of pine boughs and the serene beauty of Mendon Ponds. There, he turned on his "secret radio," searching for his spirit again in this new universe he was helping to create. Thoughts about the eternal clouds in the Rochester sky, the approaching bitter cold, drifting snow, and long winter temporarily distracted him. Rochester, however, was a town of pioneers, men and women who were wedded to ideas and ideals, among them such notables as Susan B. Anthony and Frederick Douglass. Bob wondered if these great minds had ever taken the time to walk near the ponds and the Finger Lakes in this region and recite the verse of Byron or Shelley, or to think about Emerson and the divinity of nature. He had neglected these friends for nearly a year. They had done much to give him his heart and soul in teaching.

Bob thought of his dad during his childhood days in the Bronx—often too busy working, coming home too tired to take in a ball game or silent movie. Bob was glad that he would be back in the classroom soon—an integrated class at that! He paused for a moment, feeling the crunch of a small pine cone beneath his shoe, urging his literary heroes to help him through this new experience.

In the fall of 1969, Bob taught his first integrated class at RIT. It was a required freshman course, "Language and Thought." He had firsthand knowledge of what it was like to be a deaf student enrolled in a class of hearing students, but now he was in front of the class. "I felt a new energy, and I had a new vision," he reflected, "which before I never really had. I was part of a ground-swell, and I was given the leeway to be creative and innovative."[13] This course included about thirty students, ten of them deaf. Liz O'Brien, a recently hired faculty member who had deaf parents and was a skilled signer, served as Bob's interpreter. Bob began the course with a half-hour-long Russian film with subtitles, *Ballad of Love,* a sort of "Romeo and Juliet" story. The lead character in this piece of fiction was a deaf dancer with the Moscow National Theatre of the Deaf who fell in love with a hearing violinist for a Moscow orchestra. The class was hooked on the subject matter by the film and a great discussion followed. After four decades of profound deafness, Bob knew that his voice was different. It only took a couple of days, however, before the hearing students became used to it. The ice thus broken, he had no problem from then on, anytime he was asked to teach a course at RIT. Watching Bob use signs, fingerspelling, speech, acting, and pantomime, all of his students, hearing and deaf, enjoyed his "hamming" throughout the course.

Meanwhile, he was able to bring the players from the National Theatre of the Deaf back to Rochester in 1969. John Debes, director of educational programs at Kodak in Rochester, had seen the troupe perform in 1967 at Nazareth College, and when he learned about Bob's involvement with the theater company each summer, he asked Bob over lunch if he could get the NTD to be part of the program for the 1969 National Conference on Visual Literacy held at the East Avenue Inn in Rochester. Bob worked hard to pull this off. At the conference, among the 359 people from thirty-one states, the District of Columbia, and Canada, Bob presented on "The Silent Language and the National Theatre of the Deaf" and how the deaf actors personified the language of signs and sign-mime so expressively.[14] He described David Hays's work with Broadway theatre, the O'Neill Memorial Theatre Foundation, and the founding of NTD. Toward the end of this paper, he introduced Hays, who gave a brief talk, and then several members of the NTD performed some short poems and stories. Among the actors were Bernard Bragg, Joe Velez, Linda Bove, and Marybeth Miller, with Lou Fant voice interpreting.

By this time Bernard Bragg had studied under Marcel Marceau, and his mastery of mime was superb. He was also the first professional deaf actor in and a cofounder of NTD. It was Bragg's signing of poetry and selections from Shakespeare, however, that Bob most cherished. He called Bragg "the Prince of Players on the Silent Stage" and welcomed the opportunity to assist Helen Powers, a freelance writer for the Bridgeport, Connecticut, *Sunday Post,* with her insightful biography of Bernard.

The following summer, 1970, Bob again taught at the National Theatre of the Deaf in Connecticut. Now the students came from NTID as well as Gallaudet College, California State University in Northridge, and other communities in the United States that had deaf theater programs. NTD also attracted some foreign deaf students from Finland, Sweden, Denmark, Japan, and Australia. It was a wonderful experience for Bob to see them interact and exchange ideas and share their skills. Bob collaborated with others to translate into sign language such plays as Dylan Thomas's *Under Milkwood* and Puccini's *Sganarelle*. With the demands on his time at NTID, however, Bob could only spend a few weeks at NTD during the summer sessions, offering short courses on the history of theater and creative interpretation of literature in sign language, along with selections from the *Spoon River Anthology*, by Edgar Lee Masters, and Shakespeare. It was during these weeks with NTD that he also became enamored with haiku, a Japanese three-line poem form with a specific syllable count.

Bob cherished these summer sessions as the most enjoyable and stimulating period of his professional career. He learned much from established professionals in theater, including Joe Layton and Gene Lasko, who directed Hollywood films as well as Broadway plays; and from others like Sahomi Takibana, who taught Kabuki dance and drama; David Hays, stage design; George White, president of the O'Neill Foundation, stage fencing and sword fighting; and Fred Volpel, costume design.

With the National Theatre of the Deaf in Bob's blood now, it was no surprise to Frisina when the deaf professor organized

Curtain call for NTID Drama Club actors during their first production, *Spring Fever*, April 1970.

the NTID Drama Club on a snowy winter's night in 1970, when he met with a small group of students in the Webb Auditorium on the RIT campus. More than a hundred dues-paying student members eventually joined what Bob called "the center of social life" for NTID students at RIT. The purpose of the Drama Club was to provide an outlet for creative expression for deaf students. Many other students were involved in making posters, working in the box office, and managing the business aspects of theater sales. Whether the students were majoring in engineering, art, business, or other career programs, his goal was to "give students as much hands-on experience as possible in whatever their field."[15] Shirley also proved to be a catalyst during the early years of the Drama Club, applying her talents as a mime as the students developed their skills for various performances.

Bob held high hopes for the NTID students who fell in love with theater through these dramatic sketches and plays. He also encouraged many young hearing students to become more expressive with their hands and body as well as their voices so they would be better able to get their ideas across. It was a wonderful adventure, and he enjoyed it as much as the students.

Meanwhile, Shirley had obtained a position as a librarian at the Rochester School for the Deaf. As she had done at Fanwood, she tackled the organization of the resources with great enthusiasm. Again, she searched the campus buildings for books, reports, magazines, and historical artifacts; and she glossed up and bound journals and convention proceedings for the special library for faculty and administration. Over the years to follow, Shirley established her own legacy as a librarian who encouraged deaf students to fall in love with reading.

Bob's enthusiasm about working with both deaf and hearing students soon led him to offer short courses and workshops at nearby colleges. By December 1970, he was teaching twenty theater arts majors from nearby Nazareth College and St. John Fisher College in Rochester. Shirley joined Bob for some of the classes. She was talented in pantomime and had often given performances at schools, hospitals, and clubs for the deaf. Bob hoped this effort would someday lead to a full-scale dramatics production involving both hearing and deaf students at NTID. To Bob, theater offered opportunities that significantly supported the overall learning of deaf students in the technical college. "The deaf person participating in dramatic expression gets a psychological boost which serves to remove the stigma of deafness," he reflected in 1970.[16] He believed that theater dispelled the sense of passive resignation some deaf students exhibited, and "replaces it with confidence and success."[17]

The hearing students, on the other hand, were learning to develop a greater awareness of how to communicate by methods other than the spoken word. They were projecting themselves more visually through mime, body movement, and facial expression. Bob had experience with hearing and deaf actors in the NTD summer workshops, and he was delighted to see the "embryonic cooperation" succeed in Rochester as well. The course at Nazareth emphasized pantomime and sign-mime, which was "literally painting pictures in the air." He believed that the visual imagery allowed it to be understood by hearing persons unfamiliar with sign language. "Visual alertness, a live imagination, and empathy are the only requirements needed by hearing persons to appreciate this new art form."[18]

In these short courses and workshops, Bob also used haiku, imagistic Japanese poems, to introduce the students to sign-mime. The students were asked to stand like statues on the stage while he gave each of them a poem to sign-mime. He read such verse as "Butterfly asleep / folded soft on temple bell . . . / Then the bronze gong rang!" and "A saddening world: / flowers whose sweet bloom must fall . . . / As we too, alas!" He would then analyze, interpret, and dramatize the words in signs, making the poems come to life. As the poem was read, the "statues" came to life and visually expressed the words, using only their bodies and hands. As Bob reflected on one student's performance, "What came out of her mouth [the reader's] made no sense to me, but what I saw on your faces and in the signs was poetry."[19]

To Bob's delight, Rochester had its own brand of baseball! Almost immediately after moving to town he became an avid fan of the Rochester Red Wings, Baltimore's minor league baseball team. By the spring of 1971, he was ready to bid farewell to the Yankees. He traveled to Yankee Stadium in New York City. It was the last time Bob would sit at Yankee Stadium, an experience he described to me as leaving him feeling empty as he mused on the Bronx Bombers and the ghosts of the baseball icons of his youth. Under Yankee owner George Steinbrenner, with his high-handed management, Bob's support for the team had slowly eroded. The Orioles had become his favorite team. Bob returned home to Rochester, sat down, and wrote a poem of nostalgic verse reflecting his love for the game, "Opening Day: Yankee Stadium":

Soon that new crop of grass will have concealed
Those spikeworn pathways near the bleacher wall,
And that new rookie out in center field
May blaze his own while chasing for the ball.
Yet, every cynic in the frigid throng
Senses a missing glory in the air
And yearns for one who swept the team along,
Whose every move was followed by a stare
That marveled at each scintillating catch,
At every epic swing, each classic throw
Which none could imitate with such dispatch
As Mickey Mantle and DiMaggio.
But, lo! The rookie snares one, on the wing,
The crowd goes wild . . . .and suddenly it's Spring!

Nothing Great— Without Enthusiasm

The Drama Club quickly brought attention to NTID as a new source of theater in the Rochester community. The club began with short skits put together rather quickly, with only seven to ten days of rehearsals. Mimes, dances, and songs were common. Every academic quarter, the club offered a two-hour show and hosted an annual Drama Club Awards Night. During that colorful event in 1971, the deaf students had mimeographed the program only a few minutes before the performance. After the lights went out, several hundred faculty, staff, and students enjoyed the first hour of entertainment and the awards presentations. When the lights came on for intermission, lo and behold there were many faces and hands streaked blue from the ink still wet from the programs. Long lines formed at the restroom sinks and even at the water fountains in the halls!

That was a challenging year for Bob. He lost thirty pounds after developing a hyperthyroid condition that included a nervous stomach, sensitivity to heat and cold, and eyestrain. Two different doctors failed to diagnose the subtle illness. He was not sure what was happening to him until his own mother-in-law came for a visit that summer and recognized the symptoms her brother had experienced with hyperthyroidism. After X-rays, the doctors located the problem and Bob went through therapy on a weekly basis. He nevertheless fought that illness through long hours of rehearsal to direct his first major play at NTID, *It's a Deaf, Deaf, Deaf, Deaf World.* The play included satires and poked fun at the attitude forced on young deaf people that "This is a hearing world."[1] It lampooned some of the canons of deaf education, educators, and communication. Bob adapted the theme song, which was signed by Betti Bonni, Janice Cole, and Barbara Ray, and added the featured one-act farce *The Planet of the Deaf.* Making the point that it *is* also a deaf world, the play illustrated "the universal use of pantomime, body language, silent language and other methods of communication" in many expressions and activities of hearing people.[2] In *Planet of the Deaf,* Chuck Baird portrayed the "hearie" captive forced to make decisions just to please the majority of "deafies." He falls in love with the daughter of the chief and wants to marry her. She will do so only if he becomes deaf and after taking a drug he wakes up suddenly gifted with the power to communicate in flawless sign language. As a writer in the national magazine *The Deaf American* summarized, "A hilarious scene follows in which he soliloquizes a la Hamlet: 'To hear or not to hear, that is the question!' Upon suddenly seeing the beautiful maid (Beth Bystricki), he decides, that 'speech is cheap as silver, but sign language is beautiful as that deaf girl's golden hair.'[3] In all, Bob directed fifty-five students in this production.

During the NTID Drama Club rehearsals, Bob found his own enthusiasm unharnessed. But, as with his teaching, he would often carry on a bit too long with his lessons and anecdotes. It was NTID student Chuck J. Jones who, during one Drama Club rehearsal running well past midnight, invented the "name sign" PANARA. Produced with the sign for the letter *P* and made with several hops as in exaggeration, the sign characterized Bob's tendency to enthusiastically go on and on. The name sign CJ gave to Bob was given with great affection, and it stayed with him for decades. "Although he could talk forever," CJ, now a professional actor, reminisced, "he allowed me to be creative and thus have trust in my acting. He is my role model, and a great friend."[4]

The melding of drama, literature, and poetry into a technical college environment was an accomplishment beyond what Frisina had anticipated. Building on his seminal 1945 essay, another article on deaf poets published in *The Silent Worker* in 1954, and his 1960 work on *The Silent Muse,* edited with Taras B. Denis and John McFarlane, Bob expanded Deaf Studies as a field of scholarship through several new publications, most notably the two installments of "The Deaf Writer in America from Colonial Times to 1970" in the *American Annals of the Deaf,* and "Deaf Characters in Fiction and Drama" in *The Deaf American.* In the *Annals* articles, he delved into the works of many deaf men and women, including the verse of Joseph Schuyler Long and his work on the origin and use of sign language; the creative interpretation of the fine arts by such artists as Albert Ballin and Kelly Stevens; popular magazine feature writers such as Abbie M. Watkins in the *Saturday Evening Post* and Reverend Warren M. Smaltz in the *Reader's Digest*; poets John Carlin, Laura Redden, Howard Terry, Alice McVan, and Rex Lowman; anthologists such as Taras Denis, John

McFarlane, and Bob himself; science fiction writers like Barry Miller; and "crusaders" of the "Little Paper Family," the various publications of the Deaf community. "And what of tomorrow?" Bob has asked. "And the future? Shall we live to see a deaf writer emerge from the shadow of obscurity and assume the stature of a Robert Frost or an Ernest Hemingway or a Tennessee Williams? As Shakespeare put it: 'Tis a consummation devoutly to be wished.'"[5]

In his *Deaf American* analysis of fiction and drama, Bob examined the roles of deaf characters from as far back as Daniel Defoe's *The History of the Life and Surprising Adventures of Duncan Campbell,* written in 1720, revealing a "surprising number" of deaf characters scattered throughout classic literary works. He wrote that the informed writer does not depict the deaf character as a type, but as an individual. Bob concludes "the paradox of our time is that, in the midst of our greatest achievement in methods of communication and mass media, there is a striking similarity in the problems of the deaf and the dilemma of modern man."[6] To communicate freely, he believed, is to be wholly understood.

The groundbreaking ceremony for the new NTID facilities in June 1971 was an exciting experience for Bob. With President Lyndon Baines Johnson's wife, Lady Bird Johnson, Governor Hugh L. Carey, and other distinguished guests coming to the campus, Bob was enthusiastic. They watched proudly as four deaf students broke the ground at RIT, assuring that the college would have its new facilities within a few years. It was time to celebrate, and after the spade broke ground, Bob addressed the many guests attending. He talked about how it was his good fortune to have the honor of representing the Deaf community and the deaf leadership of the profession on this occasion of breaking ground for the new facilities at this campus. "I am deeply appreciative of this opportunity and the homage that accompanies it, although I do fear that I am being honored above my merit in view of the many distinguished deaf teachers who are equally deserving and even more so."[7] More important than this token courtesy, he explained, was the fact that NTID had provided the opportunity for outstanding deaf persons to become an integral part of the institute and the community of educators at RIT. He summarized, "It is my fervent hope that this act of groundbreaking, and the ideal for which it stands, shall serve as a living model for others to emulate after our fashion, and that [quoting Shakespeare] 'in . . . many ages hence shall this our lofty scene be acted o'er In states unborn and accents yet unknown.'"[8]

In July, a month after the groundbreaking, Bob learned that his former mentor, Powrie Vaux Doctor, had passed away while attending the Sixth Congress of the World Federation of the Deaf in Paris. Bob noted that Doc had died only a few blocks away from the grave of the venerable Abbé de l'Epée, who had established the world's first government-sponsored school for deaf children. Doc had been much more than a mentor to Bob. He was a dear friend, and his death was a major blow for Bob and Shirley. As the news of Doc's death sent a flood of grief through the college community where he taught for more than four decades, Bob joined many other admiring former students in a tribute to him published in *Gallaudet Today* magazine.[9]

A few lines of Bob's commemorative portrait, "Dr. Powrie Vaux Doctor—Pro Memoria," follow:

> Instead, he chose a road less traveled by
> As "teacher of the deaf," and with a zeal
> He charted out a rainbow in the sky
> And challenged us to seek a "beau ideal,"
> So did he lead us on to high emprise—
> A mentor and a man most scholarly,
> A diplomat, and so surprising wise
> That laughter was his best philosophy,
> Renowned as all the world's ambassador,
> He was our teacher, friend, and counselor.

Bob still cherishes a book Doc had handed him as a birthday gift many years earlier, *The Gospel of Emerson*. Bob had thrived on Emerson's words, "Nothing great was ever achieved without enthusiasm."[10]

Over the next few years, the NTID facilities slowly emerged out of the swamplands at RIT. Bob could see the towering dormitory, the academic complex, and the dining commons being built beam upon beam as he entered the campus each morning. As the theater program at NTID took root under his guidance—in temporary quarters and with borrowed equipment and rented costumes as they waited for the new facilities—there was no question that Bob's work in the performing arts was leaving a positive impression in the Rochester community. Among the regulars attending the NTID Drama Club performances was Dr. Harley Parker, director of the Royal Ontario Museum in Toronto, and the first holder of RIT's Kern Chair

At the "Sound of Vision" conference at Rochester Institute of Technology in October 1973, Bob joined other experts to discuss "sensory orchestration." Left to right are Marshall McLuhan, Bob, and Harley Parker.

in Communications. Parker had coauthored with Marshall McLuhan the book *Through the Vanishing Point,* a study of space in poetry and painting, and he and Bob became friends, often having lunch together in the College Union and discussing the beauty of sign language. In the spring of 1973, Parker invited Bob and RIT Professor Richard Zakia to visit the museum, where an exhibit of Chinese art was on display.

The next day Bob had lunch with Marshall McLuhan, followed by a meeting with McLuhan's class of about fifteen students. Bob had asked Mickey Jones to accompany him as an interpreter. In class, McLuhan asked Bob to demonstrate some haiku poetry in sign-mime. He followed this with Robert Frost's "Stopping by Woods on a Snowy Evening," Emily Dickinson's "I Like to See It Lap the Miles," and e. e. cummings's "In Just Spring." The enthusiastic response from McLuhan's students included a comparison of sign language and Chinese iconography. It was a special experience for Bob to have discourse with the author of the credo that had guided him for years: Don't let the student merely read the book; let him *be* the book.

Not long after Bob's visit to Marshall McLuhan's class, Parker formalized his Kern Chair project, which included a conference held in Rochester in October 1973 with the theme "Sound of Vision." Bob was invited to be one of the leaders of the conference along with McLuhan, Eugene Mindell (author of *They Grow in Silence*), Douglas Inkster (an expert on blindness), Robert Houde (a specialist in technological aids for deaf people), Edmund S. Carpenter (a University of Pennsylvania professor of anthropology), Harley Parker, and Walter Cooper (a University of Rochester professor of chemistry and advocate of equal opportunity). The conference focused on the idea that blindness is a medium, deafness is a medium, and that people can mediate the sensory inputs unique to each state. The participants sought commonalities in "sensory orchestration." Bob delved into sign language, nonverbal communication, and parallels with Chinese ideography, which he had discussed in McLuhan's class a few months earlier. Both were "picture languages" without the phonetic basis that characterizes English. He spoke of the American poet Ezra Pound moving toward "imagism" in poetry and away from redundancy. "Modern poetry, or the 'new poetry' as you now see it shutters 'singleness' of things—the concrete object, the basic image. Signs do the same thing."[11] He mentioned how a reviewer in *Time* magazine had recently seen the National Theatre of the Deaf and remarked on the economy of sign language, "A word in hand is worth two in the mouth."[12]

The dedication of the Lyndon Baines Johnson Building in 1974 was another special moment in Bob's life. The building contained a state-of-the-art theater along with technical laboratories and classrooms. During the design phase, Frisina was well aware that the performing arts had an established tradition in the Deaf community. The theater he envisioned as part of the new facilities at RIT was both exciting and innovative. Others at first questioned the need for a formal theater at a technical college. To Frisina's credit, he would not cut corners in this area. He did not want a "cafeteria with a platform," but a genuine theater that would enrich the lives of students residing on campus as well as serving as a bridge between the greater community and the students, faculty, and staff of the new school. Frisina was a staunch patron of the theater, and he ensured that ample space was given to Bob's growing performing arts program. The new theater was designed specifically to give deaf students a chance to fully enjoy theatrical presentations as participants on stage, behind the scenes, or in the audience. The architectural details included two-way televisions connected between the stage and dressing rooms; a seating plan designed to offer a perfect view of the stage from anywhere in the theater;

Bob and Lady Bird Johnson at the ceremony naming the "Lyndon Baines Johnson Building" in October 1979 during RIT's 150th Anniversary.

a lab theater adjacent to the main stage for rehearsals, tryouts, and classes; a costume shop; an authentic "green room" in which performers could relax before and in between appearances onstage; and a scenery shop. The floors of both the lab theater and the stage were constructed of special soft pine wood to transmit vibrations. The theater's curtain was made of cotton velvet in deep purple (a background conducive to interpreting) with gold appliquéd stripes.[13]

At the ceremony, with such dignitaries as Lady Bird Johnson, Governor Hugh L. Carey, and Representative Daniel Flood looking on, Bob stood on the new stage for the first time to present a professional speech. "Dr. Frisina and I don't mince our words," he told the audience. "It's the best theater of its

Governor Hugh L. Carey and his wife Evangeline visiting NTID
in the late 1970s. Carey was a sponsor for the NTID Act of 1965.
William E. Castle, NTID director, is second from left.

kind in the world, for the simple reason that it is custom-made
exclusively for the deaf. . . . Each and every one of us has reason to rejoice in this happy reunion of our . . . alumni which
rekindles our early faith in NTID of the promise of individual
fulfillment that it holds for the young deaf adult of tomorrow."[14]

But the dedication of the NTID facilities was a bittersweet
experience for Bob. Although he had planted the seed for educational theater at the college, at the very time this new theater was being dedicated, he was at a crossroads in his career,
devoting his time almost exclusively to teaching in the RIT
College of General Education. "I closed the curtain to the theater experience with the realization that I finally had come full

circle," he said. "I now could devote all my time and energy to teaching integrated classes in literary studies within the College of Liberal Arts—which was my original goal in leaving Gallaudet for NTID. That, and the opportunity to promote Deaf Studies through research and writing. The result brought a rich and fulfilling end to the academic life and my career as a teacher."[15] Bob had expanded his course offerings to include Shakespeare, great world drama, modern poetry, and the contemporary American novel, incorporating material from Deaf Studies whenever he could. The students praised his teaching. "Fantastic!" one said, "His classes are so great! I really enjoy learning from him!" Another said that Bob "really teaches you to understand and appreciate literature . . . his classes are very exciting!"[16]

It was not easy for Bob to let go of theater, but he had ambitious plans for Deaf Studies in general and for teaching integrated classes at RIT. In the short time he had been working with the Drama Club, Bob had directed scores of performances at local public and private organizations, several on local television stations, five for national and state organizations, and six for special functions on campus. One of the final performances Bob directed at WORK-TV, in 1974, was called "Haiku Harvest," in which five NTID students from the Drama Club appeared on stage with an easel with haiku written on large cards in English as they signed the poetry.

The NTID Drama Club, under the coordination of David Hagans and his staff, soon evolved into a new program called Experimental Educational Theatre (EET). Now that the group had access to a facility that could offer theatrical presentations of all kinds, the EET offered an outlet for student self-expression, one that could refine and expand deaf students' communication skills and help them achieve a higher level of personal, social, and cultural development. Building on Bob's pioneering efforts, new courses in the history of the theater, translation, oral interpretation, and acting classics were developed and these, too, emphasized the learning of language and culture. The production of plays within the RIT campus and throughout the community further stimulated social interaction between the deaf and hearing students, faculty, and staff. Work training projects in stagecraft involved deaf students' majoring in areas such as fine and applied arts, electrical engineering, graphic arts, and the applied sciences.[17]

Bob was delighted to see that the first production staged in the new theater in the Lyndon Baines Johnson building was Shakespeare's *The Taming of the Shrew,* which he had adapted into sign language. He felt much satisfaction in having founded the NTID dramatics program, and now that it was under the capable control of his colleagues, Bob could delight in his former drama students becoming professionals, some pursuing theater as a result of their involvement in the Drama Club during its early years. Even if the theater he had initiated was, in his own words, "only my hobby," he wrote, "I feel good to know that quite a few of my students became professional actors for NTD, the Fairmount Theatre [in Cleveland], and other places."[18]

Along with his courses, Bob kept himself busy with a renewed interest in Deaf Studies. He had fresh hope that the academic life for which he had longed had finally arrived. During those first six years of growing pains, he had changed job titles numerous times. He had moved into his first office at the RIT downtown campus in 1967 and then relocated to the new campus when it opened in April 1968. First he was located in the College of Science, then in the College of General Studies Building. For several years his office was in a temporary building while he served as head of the NTID English Department, and when Frisina needed Bob's help in planning the new buildings and programs, Bob moved again to an office in a dormitory!

The 1974–1975 school year ended with several memorable events for Bob. In the spring, the Rochester Institute of Technology presented him with the Eisenhart Award for Outstanding Teaching. He had been nominated by the students, and a committee had selected him for this great honor. Sadly, Doc, who had initially encouraged Bob to consider a career as a teacher, had died several years earlier.

Graduation at RIT was followed by a whirlwind year. In August, John Panara married Janis Attaldo, a girl from Rochester. Shortly after the wedding, Bob began a one-year leave of absence to teach Deaf Studies and other courses in literature and writing at the California State University at Northridge (CSUN). He had also arranged with Bill Castle to bring Sahomi Takibana, the Kabuki teacher and dance performer, to join the theater staff at NTID as an artist in residence for half a year, directing a Kabuki play and teaching Kabuki drama and dance. With the newlyweds John and Janis living in their home for the next nine months, Bob, Shirley, and their dog Spotty, flew to Los Angeles at the end of August.

Bob remained in California for the entire school year, during which he taught English composition, literature, and theater history. As at RIT, his courses at CSUN gave the hearing students a heightened awareness of deafness and deaf people. They enjoyed new insights into the image and function of deaf characters in literature and learned how these characterizations are sometimes symbolic of the condition of modern man. Bob's courses also helped the deaf students discover their roots in tracing the achievements of notable deaf Americans and their contributions to the economic, social, and cultural growth of America.

After commencement in June 1976, and enriched by his experience in California, the family returned to the Rochester clouds and the bitter winter snows, but also to the twin joys of family—John and Janis—and the NTID. Before heading home, however, Bob was faced with yet another difficult decision. He had been offered a full-time position by Ray Jones, founding director of the CSUN Center on Deafness and the Leadership Training Program, to remain there and teach. But NTID was in Bob's blood now, and he turned down the offer. Indeed he found it good to be back as he took in a few Red Wings games that summer and let the tempting offer to remain in California fade into memory.

Over the next two years, time passed quickly at NTID, and before they knew it, Bob and Shirley became grandparents, when Janis gave birth to a son, William, on June 1, 1978. When Bob first saw Billy, he and Shirley were overjoyed. "Now I can play catch with another future little leaguer!" he told Shirley. When their second grandchild, Erin, was born on

John and Janis Panara with Bob and Shirley's grandchildren, Bill and Erin.

August 29, 1980, Shirley cradled the baby in her arms and said, to Bob, "Now I can teach another future little leaguer to pitch and bat!"[19] John joined the faculty at NTID in 1978. He was responsible for providing notetaking and tutoring support to deaf students mainstreamed with hearing students in RIT courses. Within a short time, he joined the Liberal Arts Support Team, teaching courses in writing and literature. He had recently completed his master's degree in English, and found himself "immersed in literature." "Without a doubt," John reflected, "my interest in literary studies could be traced to my father's influence."

During John's youth he had been exposed to lyrical and narrative poetry, growing up with a father who would spontaneously recite lines. In addition, his father always had been a great storyteller, whether recounting personal experiences or works of fiction, so John learned to appreciate the power of the

narrative form. Later, when he was a college student, his professors reminded him of his father, brimming with a passion for
literature that was nothing short of inspirational. John reflected:

> I liked the way in which my professors functioned as a kind
> of magnifying glass, helping students gain insight into the text.
> It is an analogy my father liked to use. And, like my father, my
> professors were great communicators who connected easily
> with students. I had decided that I wanted to do the same with
> deaf students. It seemed a logical step because I had both the
> communication skills and a bond with deaf people that tran-
> scended my connection to most hearing people. So, getting
> involved in teaching English to deaf students was something
> that came very naturally to me.[20]

As he taught full-time in the College of Liberal Arts and
served as a faculty member on the Liberal Arts Support Team
to tutor deaf students in integrated classes, Bob continued to
design new Deaf Studies courses based on his research on deaf
writers, poets, and the roles of deaf characters in fiction and
drama. In his classes, he covered such topics as characters feign-
ing deafness in Sir Walter Scott's "The Talisman" (1825) and
"Peverill of the Peak" (1831); deaf characters as "freaks," such
as Lewis Wallace's "The Prince of India" (1893); accurate por-
trayals of nineteenth-century views on successful education efforts with deaf persons (e.g., Wilkie Collins's "Hide and Seek,"
1861, and Charles Dickens's "Dr. Marigold," 1900); and a portrait of loneliness in Ivan Turgenev's "Mumu" (1852). Watching Bob on video teaching "Mumu" is a classic illustration of

his ability to encourage his deaf students to find a larger meaning in the story. The tale is about a deaf groundskeeper who is
in love with a woman, but who is frustrated by a dowager's attempt to escape her own loneliness by controlling his fate. Bob
discusses Gerasm, the deaf giant of a man, who is laughed at
because of his problems with speech. Through sign and mime,
Bob shows the emotions of the characters in the story. At the
end of the discussion he asks, "Why can we call Gerasm a "deaf
giant" in a symbolic, not realistic, way?" Through the dialogue
with his students, they come to realize that Gerasm symbolizes
the same problem many hearing serfs experienced in this era of
Russian history. "Gerasm symbolizes their oppression," Bob
explained. "By making him deaf, Turgenev stresses the theme
of oppression and obedience in all the lower classes in the
Tsarist regime."

Bob began supplementing his Deaf Studies work by docu-
menting the successes of deaf athletes. Earlier, in 1975, at the
commencement of the Model Secondary School for the Deaf
in Washington, D.C., among the "giants in their field of work"
that Bob held up graduates as models, leaders, or "inspiration
for you to follow," was professional baseball player William
Ellsworth "Dummy" Hoy, the "Mighty Mite," who was light-
ning fast on his feet.[21] ("Dummy" was a common nineteenth-
century nickname for deaf people who did not use much
speech.) In the process another seed was planted in Bob's
mind—reading up on Hoy for this commencement address
started Bob on a thirty-year crusade to have the deaf baseball
player inducted into the Baseball Hall of Fame at Cooperstown.
Hoy was the first deaf person to become a superstar in the
game, and he is believed to have invented the hand signals still

used today by umpires for calling strikes and balls. In Bob's youth his heroes in the hearing world were many: Tony Lazzeri, Babe Ruth, Joe DiMaggio, Esther Williams, and Johnny Weissmuller, among others. Later, he idolized Brooks Robinson and Cal Ripken. After he became deaf, however, he also began acquiring heroes in the deaf world, including boxers Marvin Marshall, who had been a college mate at Gallaudet, and Gene Silent Hairston; and baseball players Dummy Hoy and Luther "Dummy" Taylor, who pitched for John McGraw's New York Giants.[22]

In the late 1970s and early 1980s, Bob conducted a series of interviews with such notables as Bernard Bragg for the NTID Interpreter Training Program videotape series and produced other videotapes with such titles as "Sign Mime, the Art of Visual Imagery." He was recognized nationally for his role as an advocate/promoter, writer, founder, director, and adapter of plays: he received the Humanitarian Award in Theatre of the Deaf from Gallaudet College (1977) and the Service Award for Contributions to the Humanities by the Deaf Hollywood television and film production company *Beyond Sound* (1981). The latter award served as further impetus to argue for more Deaf Studies courses at the college level. In 1982, he proposed that a new course, Deaf Heritage, be offered at RIT. One of the objectives was to increase awareness of the cultural heritage of deaf people by studying their contributions in literature, theater, film, the arts, and the sciences. The course included not only regular classes, but also evening sessions with motion pictures and videotapes, and attendance at any special productions of the NTID Educational Theatre and National Theatre of the Deaf was required. In 1983, he published an article further advocating Deaf Studies. "Cultural Arts among Deaf People" summarizes the importance of Deaf Studies as a field, stressing how this work can both increase "Deaf Awareness" among the general public, and offer models to inspire younger deaf people. In Bob's view, the study of accomplished deaf people makes it possible to discover a "new image" of one's self as a person with self-worth, with greater confidence, with a more positive attitude toward life and society. And the more one studies this new image, the stronger becomes one's desire to seek other examples, of deaf persons who have succeeded in the various cultural arts.[23] *Great Deaf Americans,* coauthored with his son, John, was also published in 1983. Shirley ardently supported them, typing, editing, indexing, and arguing for the inclusion of deaf women she felt were deserving of more attention.

The novel *Roots* by Alex Haley and its dramatization on national television in the 1970s had created more awareness of "the black experience" in America than any other single work since 1852, when Harriet Beecher Stowe published *Uncle Tom's Cabin.* Unlike *Uncle Tom's Cabin, Roots* was the work of a black author, and black people played the leading roles on television. To Bob, this was a cultural breakthrough, which had great significance in terms of how deaf people might also undertake more relevant roles in defining their own past as well as their destiny. Bob's focus on the accomplishments of deaf people was a hallmark of his professional writing and ran counter to the spate of books published by others in the field of Deaf education that emphasized pathology first and later, victimhood (and likely had a larger market). It was his research and writing on Deaf authors and Deaf culture—his "labor amoris" (labor of love)—and his attempt to develop an awareness of our Deaf heritage and help perpetuate it, that inspired him to write. He showed through his publications and presentations and his teaching that deaf persons had blazed new pathways for others to follow in the theater, in television, and in film. The increased awareness of the "Deaf experience" in these fields opened the minds of employers and educators in the mainstream and inspired others to follow in Bob's footsteps in writing books and articles about deaf visual artists, scientists, and those in other professional and technical fields.

In the relatively short time span of fifteen years, the National Theatre of the Deaf and the hard work of many deaf actors had transformed the image of what deaf people could do in performing arts. Almost single-handedly, Bob had kept NTID, despite its status as a technical college, integrally involved in this movement over much of its first decade. He also introduced many of RIT's hearing students to the world of deafness for the first time when they came to the university, and some of these students went on to pursue the performing arts after graduation. Amazingly enough, Bob did not consider himself unusually outgoing. "I am not an extrovert," he told John Lee Clark in an interview for *The Tactile Mind,* a quarterly that promotes sign language literature. "All the years after deafness I spent hours and hours at home alone. . . . I learned to enjoy my solitude. This didn't impede my social life."[24]

In the classroom, however, something happened. Bob assumed the character of the people in the stories he told. He was able to build up good rapport even with those who were not particularly interested in the subject matter. This talent reflects

Bob's ability to draw from his inner life and focus externally on the characters he presents in his teaching. Theater actor-directors such as Konstantin Stanislavsky have discussed how many great actors have this ability.

Jean Worth, who learned sign language as a resident advisor in a dormitory at RIT, was the first hearing person to join the NTID Drama Club. Bob believed that her contributions represented "an important step toward the integration and social interaction between deaf and hearing students at RIT."[25] The NTID Drama Club awarded Worth the "Best Newcomer" award in 1971. By 1981, she had become an artist and aspiring actress, a Metropolitan Museum tour guide, and a sign language consultant and interpreter. She interpreted director John Stone's instructions for *Sesame Street* deaf cast member Linda Bove. Worth credited Bob with having a strong influence on her during her college years. "He's fabulous, so alive! . . . If Bob Panara hadn't taken such an interest in me, I never would have gone to summer school at the National Theatre of the Deaf."[26]

In his quest to establish Deaf Studies as a field, Bob felt that deaf students should study the works of deaf authors as poets, novelists, dramatists, and biographers who have preserved some record of the life and work of deaf persons who have succeeded in the arts. There were now several resources to assist teachers, including Florence Crammate's 1975 work in editing Reverend Guilbert Braddock's series of short biographies titled *Notable Deaf Persons,* and Jack Gannon's definitive narrative history, *Deaf Heritage,* in 1981. With so many new challenges at the new college of NTID in the late 1960s,

Bob had been unable to finish his Ph.D. dissertation at Catholic University, titled "Deaf Characters in Literature and Drama." His book *Great Deaf Americans,* coauthored with his son, John, was the capstone to his lifelong commitment to Deaf Studies.

Being and Reading

In a 1974 video of Bob teaching the elements of poetry, he asks his class to read John Masefield's "The West Wind." He guides them toward an understanding of alliteration in the first line: "It's a warm wind, the west wind, full of birds' cries." They discuss their own experiences in using their senses to feel wind and, for some students, to hear the cries of birds. He dramatizes being there, smelling the daffodils. They discuss similes when they reach the second line of the second stanza, "Apple orchards blossom there, and the air's like wine." How would a child interpret "the air's like wine"? Bob asks, encouraging them to think about language and thought and how experience plays a role in interpreting a poem. "Do you smell anything?" he follows as his class reads, "It's April, and blossom time, and white is the may." By the time the class finishes the poem, the students not only know how to use their senses to analyze a poem, but how to *be* there in the countryside, realizing the full meaning of "spring" and "spring fever."

Bob then examines a line from Alfred Lord Tennyson's "My life has crept so long on a broken wing." He asks a student to act out the word "crept" so that the whole class senses the slow and careful nature of the movement. And in advancing through additional lines, the students become part of the verse. Whether it is Bob or the students acting out the lines to construct meaning, there are smiles on all their faces.

Perhaps the greatest characteristic of Bob's exemplary teaching was his emphasis on the verb "to be." Today there is research supporting student-centered "active," "participative," or "interactive" approaches. But this was "old hat" for Bob, who developed this mode of teaching through intuition and experience. He had always believed in emphasizing the *involvement* of students in the classroom. Over the years, he had collected several dictums that defined his teaching. Influenced by Marshall McLuhan's *The Medium Is the Message,* Bob encouraged his students not only to read a book, but *be* the book. Another influence came from Archibald MacLeish's "Ars Poetica": "A poem should not mean / But be." Bob saw poetry as being much more than words with aesthetic qualities. Poetry, to him, is one of the best means for communicating ideas, enlarging vocabulary, and teaching language. In 1979, he published an article titled "On Teaching Poetry to the Deaf (Or: Let the Student Be the Poem!)" in the *American Annals of the Deaf.* In arithmetic, he argued, children learn such terminology as "add," "subtract," "multiply," and "divide." In geography, they learn "latitude" and "longitude" and many other terms. But, he lamented, teachers have not been trained well to use poetry in the earlier grades to help the students develop a critical vocabulary as well as an appreciation for verse. "Once that happens," he explained, "there's no limit as to where they may go. And it stretches their imagination, enhances their sensitivity to beauty or artistry of written expression."[1] He wrote:

Why teach poetry? For the very same reason that we teach *the language arts* . . . it helps to stimulate creativity and self expression, and it encourages the development of a student's intellectual faculties—imagination, thinking, and interpretation. . . . As in exposure to dramatics or dancing, it makes students react emotionally and sensitively to artistry of expression. . . . Through the language of poetry, students can learn to perceive how the commonplace is made to seem uncommon, how old words can be expressed with freshness, originality, and beauty.[2]

Haiku provided Bob with another avenue through which to combine poetry with drama. He gave many presentations and workshops at schools for deaf students. In general, he performed haiku poetry on a variety of topics such as "Hail," "Fireworks," and "Flowers," which were met with creative and enthusiastic response. In showing how the students can "be" the poem, Bob would first take a haiku like the following by Shisea-Jo, titled "Umbrella": "As I walk in the winter rain / The umbrella / Pushes me back." He asked his students to imitate the action of the speaker in the poem. In this case, he had them hold an imaginary umbrella in hand. On their first try, they inevitably ended up stumbling backwards, holding the umbrella behind them at a sharp angle, as if the wind was pulling them back. He discussed with them what the poem says about pushing, what kind of wind it is, and how to represent this poem accurately. They must point the umbrella into the very face of the wind, he explained. In this example Bob illustrated the development of language skills, as well as thinking skills, with his student-centered approach. "This is the essence of learning," he stressed, "if we are to get at the very root of the Latinate term *educare,* meaning 'to draw out or from' the learner."[3]

When people walked into a class or workshop Bob was giving, they quickly saw how he demanded that the students "be the book" as the characters in the story or play became animated and real. His signing of Edgar Allan Poe's "The Cask of Amontillado" was as intriguing as the story of revenge itself. Bob's classroom was his stage, but his students were actors, too. This was the mission of another course he designed, "Creative Interpretation of Literature in Sign Language," which he had taught at the National Theatre of the Deaf summer sessions. For Bob, the verb "to be" was focused on the students and dialogue—not the monologue of lectures. Bob saw the "act" in "active" and "interactive" not just as an emphasis on involvement of students. He also saw it in a dramatic sense. This emphasis, too, was what drove Bob to establish the Drama Club at NTID to "give students as much hands-on experience as possible in whatever their field."[4] This is why Bob's students frequently commented on his "come-alive classroom."[5]

"A poem communicates its meaning," Bob wrote, "by the total impression it makes upon the five senses. The greater our involvement and responsiveness, the more meaningful the poem becomes and the deeper our appreciation. It is the teacher's responsibility to make this happen—to twang the five-stringed lyre within each student and turn them on with all kinds of vibrations. This is the essence of learning."[6] Bob always sought to "get rid of the paper work" in class and to focus on such facets as the aesthetics of verse. He encouraged the students to dramatize the subtleties of their own poetry through sign language and mime. It was a challenge he accepted enthu-siastically.[7] He would describe "circles of meaning" as a means of getting his students to delve more deeply into verse. He would analyze, for example, the rippling, multilayered mean-ing of the line "I have miles to go before I sleep" in Robert Frost's poem "Stopping by Woods on a Snowy Evening," and in so doing, he would reveal part of his own life philosophy: that as long as a person is alive, there is more to learn and more to do.

Bob's use of dramatization in teaching was influenced by the people he had met over the years. At CSUN, he had inter-acted with actress Nanette Fabray, and afterwards stage and screen star Vivica Lindfors was impressed with a presentation he gave on sign-mime at the National Conference of American College Theatre Arts Association at Maryland University. He had a lively discussion with her and other participants. During earlier years at the NTD Summer School, Bob had always en-joyed mingling with celebrities. David Hays had brought stage and screen star Celeste Holm to the O'Neill Memorial Theatre Center to speak. Bob had already met her at her farm home when he used to babysit for his cousin Gilda at her summer home near Hackettown, New Jersey, and Celeste was delighted to see Bob again and learn about the NTD theater work. That year, he also had met Robert Cummings at the Americana Hotel in Rochester, where he invited the actor to come and see deaf actors perform. Cummings stayed afterwards and met the students and signed autographs. Jane Fonda was also a guest at NTID in 1974, and Bob enjoyed meeting her.

One of Bob's NTID students, Karen Beiter, currently on the faculty, recalls the act of "being" in a literature course. The class was discussing a science fiction story about a robot who developed human characteristics that included being able to compose musical compositions. Eventually the robot realizes he is too intelligent and that he exceeds the creative qualities reserved for humans, and he decides to revert to the original role for which he was designed. "Being a typically orally-raised person that I was back then," Beiter remembered, "I presented the story in sign language the best I could without much dramatization. Bob Panara took the same story and dramatized it visually so well that I never forgot how he played the role of the robot and suddenly, at the end, he stopped his piano playing and went back to vacuuming duties with a blank expression again."[8] Beiter especially remembered a discussion in one of Bob's classes about how to improve Deaf education. They defined an "ideal classroom" for deaf students. Unlike what most deaf students experience today in the mainstream, this "ideal" class would be half hearing and half deaf. Everyone would sign. Educational expectations would be equal for everyone, with high standards. There would be no feeling of isolation in this bilingual/bicultural environment. "There were so many benefits to this concept," she recalled, "that when I was in the running for a pageant a few months later, a similar question came up and I had a well-thought-out answer ready and ended up winning the pageant! Bob Panara did have a very positive influence on my life and I thank him for that."[9]

Jackie Schertz, now a docent at the Memorial Art Gallery in Rochester, took three of Bob's courses from him, including creative interpretation of literature in sign language, great world drama, and deaf characters in fiction, film, and drama. In each of those classes, Schertz knew she was in for wonderful entertainment, more than would be provided by a lecture. "He was a master storyteller," she explained. "He knew the stories by heart. He became the characters in the stories. He taught in a joyous manner, without drilling." But Schertz smiled as she recalled also experiencing firsthand the tendency that led to Bob's name sign being given to him by Chuck Jones in the Drama Club. As she reminisced, "Almost always, Bob would run overtime. This invariably presented a problem for his students getting out of the classroom for their next class. Students often crowded the doorway and the hallway as they waited to get into the classroom."[10]

Bob admits that had he not developed his talent for writing verse himself, his work would have held less meaning to him and his students. His son, John, recognized that one of his father's greatest assets as a teacher was his uncanny ability to make words come alive for his students. For some deafened people, one's own voice was the sole reminder of what speech was like, and as the years pass, the recollection of the voices of others fades away. John remembered frequently waking up on Saturday mornings to the sounds of his father reciting lines. Those from Coleridge's "Kubla Khan" sparked his imagination. Words from Blake's "The Tyger" evoked a haunting beauty. When asked once what his greatest joy was as a teacher, Bob responded, "I guess it's impossible to top Longfellow's three-word statement, saying that the purest triumph of a storyteller happens when they [the students] cry, 'Tell me more!'" In teaching day in and day out over the years, he developed a philosophy similar to the old "on-with-the-show" adage of the stage. He saw teaching as being the leading character in the same play that is performed, day in and out, year after year. In order to

stay on his toes to try to feel fresh and keep the students enthralled, he would single out one or more students in the class
and play up to them, with the thought that they were seeing
him teach or perform for the first time.

Jackie Schertz also remembered the discussions she had
with Bob about the assignments for class. "We often talked
about how the themes and symbols applied to our lives," she
told me. "During those times, I saw the philosopher in him.
We were blessed with Bob Panara's wit, humor, wisdom,
warmth, generous nature, and friendship."[11]

Some teachers emphasize understanding a poem, expecting
their students to read the poem and then discuss it. They would
ask the students to write short answers to questions written on
a sheet along with the poem, "as if that is all there is to appre-
ciating and understanding the poem."[12] Bob believed that the
teacher should present the poem first on a literal level; then students can attempt to sign-mime the verse. In this way the main
idea is discovered naturally but gradually, and subsequently, the
students go into the aesthetics of the poetry, including an appreciation of the sound effects—rhyme, rhythm, alliteration—
and the visual imagery. Analyzing a poem, to Bob, was similar
in some ways to applying the scientific method. It was discovery learning at its best!

The poetry patterns of many young deaf students are often in free verse, and to foster their creative efforts Bob felt it
was important to encourage students to read more poetry to
strengthen their skill, just as one would practice baseball or
dancing. By reading various kinds of poetry, they should learn
the intricacies of metaphor, simile, alliteration, and other dimensions of verse. "I believe the final product is still somewhat

like an uncut diamond. The teacher has the duty to help them with the mechanics of English to try to make it as literate as possible." Style, to Bob, develops with time and practice, and a poet, deaf or hearing, has a particular medium for saying what he or she thinks and feels.

Then there was Emerson's guiding principle about enthusiasm that became just as much Bob's trademark as his name sign. "The trick is to have a lot of enthusiasm in what you do," he later explained, "and let it rub off on the students. Plus . . . dramatizing the material in a way that excites them, then getting them to respond."[13] Too, in his interview with Bruce White for the journal *Teaching English to Deaf and Second Language Students* in 1984, he quoted the English writer John Dryden with a related principle—the importance of "teaching delightfully."[14] As Bob told John Clark during an interview about his career, "The rapt attention and wide-eyed look of wonder is satisfaction and reward enough to believe that Cicero was right in saying that 'Teaching is the noblest profession.'"[15]

In 2003, Bob's former student Willy Conley, who became chairman of Gallaudet University's theater department, wrote, acted, and directed a video adaptation of excerpts from *Tuesdays with Morrie* as part of Gallaudet's convocation program called "Building Our Community." Following the video presentation about the charismatic professor Morrie Schwartz, who died of Lou Gehrig's disease, Conley was asked to give a speech, which led him to look back on his own experiences as a student as well as his role as a teacher. He sent me an excerpt from this speech, which mentions Bob:

> Buried deep in my memory was a drama professor who made a significant impact on me. his name was Dr. Robert Panara.

I will always remember our lunch together in his favorite restaurant several years after I graduated from R.I.T. Like Morrie, he loved to eat—but thankfully, he didn't spray food out of his mouth while talking. He was Deaf, and could eat politely with his mouth closed while signing fluently. One of the most profound things he said to me was: "in the classroom, a teacher should be educationally delightful." He was not a stage actor by profession but the classroom became his stage. He acted his heart out with his teachings. What he meant was that as teachers we must "delight" our student with learning. Panara's job was not merely to entertain or to teach us things that were easy and superficial, but to engage us in learning . . . to be delighted in the process. Professor Panara delighted me and I learned.[16]

Teaching delightfully did not mean grading lightly, however. Gerry Buckley, now an assistant vice president for college advancement at NTID, received his only C grade in his college years from Bob. "I deserved it fully," he remembers. He was enrolled in "Deaf Studies in Literature" in the 1970s, and Bob gave an assignment to analyze a story in terms of the accuracy of portrayal of a deaf character. Buckley didn't put in his best effort, writing a formal paper in a colloquial style, and Bob knew he was capable of writing much better. "Bob was always seeking to push students to live up to their full potential in the theater, in the classroom, and in their lives. He accepted no less from them and continually demonstrated to us through his work the value of this work ethic."[17]

During all his years growing up, Bob's son, John, recalled, he never once heard his father speak negatively about a student or a student's writing: "His heart just wouldn't let him do such a thing." John remembers an article written by Alex

Haley, in which he advised, "Find the good—and praise it."[18] When it came to his deaf students, his father always found a way to do just that. Of course, Bob handed out his share of low grades. It was never easy for him. Not every student could hit the ball into the seats. He could only offer to be the best batting coach he could be and hope that they would break out of a slump.

Willy Conley recalled Bob's course on deaf characters in literature and film. Bob gave his students creative writing assignments that allowed them to find the Deaf experience within each of them. Conley wrote about his medical photography internship that dealt with photographing open-heart surgery in an environment where there were no interpreters and he could not lipread the surgeons and nurses because they were wearing face masks. "Bob gave me an A," Willy remembered, "and encouraged me to submit it to R.I.T.'s literary magazine. I ended up garnering my first publication, which led to an ongoing love for creative writing."[19]

Bob often used a bilingual approach to evaluating learning in his classes. He would give students the opportunity to demonstrate their mastery of the course objectives and the ability to express themselves through the printed word (English) or in sign language (ASL or sign-mime). Students taking his 1982 course "Great World Drama," for example, could choose to do either a dramatic sketch or a written essay as a final project. Among his students' choices for dramatization were a dialogue from *The Hairy Ape* and a monologue from *The Glass Menagerie*. The written reports included essays titled "Commedia dell'Arte: An Overview" and "Renaissance Theatre: New Stage Designs."

Jackie Schertz reflected on the engaging approach Bob used in class: "After we gave our 'performances' by reciting monologues or teaming up with class members to do scenes as part of our assignments, he gave us feedback on a positive note and demonstrated ways we can improve. He created an environment that made us want to get involved. He combined the best of both old-fashioned traditional and modern innovative ways."[20]

Bob's students could also express themselves through other art forms. One student chose to model costumes in miniature for *Oedipus Rex,* while another developed a stage set model for *The Glass Menagerie.* As with his courses on poetry, Bob based his evaluations on accuracy of interpretation, translation of the printed word (script, verse, etc.) to signed form, coherence, creativity, and emotional impact.

The notion of making verse "come to life" through sign language also brought Bob into contact with the internationally known poet Allen Ginsberg, who was invited to meet with him at RIT in 1984. Articles in the Rochester newspapers welcomed the poet laureate of the Beat Generation, reminding readers that the political activist had been arrested several times for his antiestablishment protests, and that he was a self-styled "gay, Buddhist-Jewish peaceful poet in a hyper-military landscape."[21] Bob looked forward to this exchange with Ginsberg.

Some people who attended the workshop had expected Ginsberg to simply come read his poetry, and they were pleasantly surprised that he had come to learn about deafness and signing as a means of enlivening his own poetry. They first discussed Bob's experience as a person who had once heard as a child

In 1984, RIT invited the beat poet Allen Ginsberg to discuss poetry. Left to right are Jim Cohn (coordinator), Kip Webster (sign language interpreter), Ginsberg, and Bob.

and how this affected his ability to interpret poetry. Pat Graybill, deaf from birth and also on the faculty at NTID, was also there, and he described his own concept of poetry. Graybill explained that he enjoyed reciting poetry in sign, "but I don't know its rhythm." Ginsberg and Bob discussed with Graybill how this might mean he saw poetry as a "picture and an idea." As Ginsberg explained, "That's what most twentieth-century poetry is—ideas in the forms of pictures. Two of the greatest 'Imagist' poets are William Carlos Williams and Ezra Pound. There's a tendency to develop an international poetical style without rhythm and rhyme, but with harder and clearer *pictures*."[22] Through their discussion of how signing poetry was like "painting pictures in the air," Bob and Ginsberg agreed that a performance of poetry becomes pantomime or "poetry in motion"—another art form like dance. Bob got an up-close understanding of what one of the most famous, and eccentric, of the Beat Poets was like.[23]

The real fun began when Ginsberg read several of his own poems, including "Howl," with its "pornographic" verse and abstract terms like "Angelheaded hipsters," "Starry dynamo," and "Hydrogen juke box." The deaf actor Pat Graybill attempted to translate by miming the words for "music," "box," "coin from pocket," "vertical record becoming horizontal," "needle going around," "thunder shaking," and "bomb exploding."

"That looks like it, that's good!" Ginsberg said excitedly. "There's a logical jump in that whole other picture—that's interesting!"[24] Jim Cohn, who had invited Ginsberg to meet Bob, recalled the use of ASL to sign "hydrogen jukebox" as an "extra-linguistic moment that verified the sonic quality of images."[25]

Bob reflected that the workshop with Ginsberg was "the kind of happening I've often dreamed of—the opportunity to have a dialog with a distinguished poet, and to demonstrate signed poetry as a totally different mode of expression."[26]

Defining Moments

Throughout the 1980s, Bob's honors piled up. In 1985 MacMurray College in Illinois presented him with an honorary doctorate of public service at its commencement exercises. In 1986 William Castle was especially pleased to have the opportunity to announce at the banquet for an NTID/Gallaudet College English Teachers Conference that Bob would receive the honorary doctorate at Gallaudet College's commencement that May. Castle had worked for several years with Gallaudet College to encourage officials to give thought to honoring Bob in that manner. The ceremony at Gallaudet College was a special thrill for Bob.

Nothing thrilled Bob more, however, than to see his former students excel. Bernard Bragg had become the "Prince of Players on the Silent Stage." Allen Sussman, another of Bob's stars on the Fanwood stage, excelled in both psychology and writing. He had carried his talents to Gallaudet, acting in plays and taking leading roles in student life and government, and later earned a Ph.D. Suleiman Bushnaq, whom Bob had tutored after school privately at Fanwood, also attended Gallaudet and then earned a Ph.D., as did Eugene Bergman, who became a

In 1986, Bob received an honorary doctoral degree from his alma mater, Gallaudet College.

Gallaudet English professor and distinguished writer. Seymour Bernstein became an outstanding teacher at the California School for the Deaf in Riverside. Peter Shuart and Joseph Cohen did well in federal government work; Albert Berke worked with the Commission on Deafness in Connecticut and served as vice president of the National Association of the Deaf. These were sweet memories for Bob, who recalled how difficult it had been for a deaf person to earn a doctorate a few decades earlier.

Among his NTID students, Janice Cole and Betti Bonni entered the National Theatre of the Deaf as performers, as did Paul Johnston and Mike Lamitola. The latter two also became theater instructors and directors. After his NTD experience Willy Conley went on to write and teach theater at Gallaudet. Ricky Smith became a professional mime. Chuck Jones toured for years as the "Human Cartoon." The deaf artist and actor Chuck Baird recalled that his theater experience at NTID "created a sense of crystallization among the student performers . . . that pulled me into the theater world. Being able to travel and communicate about the world around us was wonderful."[1] Baird had begun his involvement in theater when Bob asked him to perform a "silly skit." After that, he took on the challenges of reciting poetry in American Sign Language, acting in plays, and, eventually, became an award-winning artist. Many of Bob's former students kept in touch with him as the years passed. Jan Afzelius, who studied under Bob in 1959 and became an active artist for one of Sweden's largest newspapers, wrote to Bob: "I can never forget you as a wonderful teacher [in poetry] during my study. A more instinctively easy-going scholar had I never enjoyed despite my low marks."[2] Gerald DeCoursey, a Gallaudet graduate (in 1958) who also took a graduate course Bob taught in 1982 at the University of Rochester, paraphrased Winston Churchill in describing Bob, "Never before have so many found so much good in one person."[3]

As Bob approached the age of sixty-five, his joy in teaching never abated, but he began to tire. Bob had looked forward to a life without deadlines, schedules, homework, and committee meetings. As he wrote a few years earlier to his friend and fellow poet Rex Lowman, "So many worlds, so much to do / So little time, so little done. There, in a nutshell (or "two-liner") Tennyson expressed the timeless and universal hang up of all people like us—who bite off more than we can chew."[4] After Bob's father passed away at the venerable age of ninety-seven at his home in Boynton Beach, in 1986, his mother moved in with his sister, Eleanor, and her family in Atlanta. She died the following year. Along with all the normal feelings of grief and loss, the death of his father and mother made Bob all the more aware of the decades marching on.

Bob retired from NTID in June of 1987. It was time to repay Shirley with closer companionship for all those times he had been absent because of rehearsals and professional activities. At this time, he looked back on his career and contributions with much pride. He had seen thousands of deaf students meet the challenge of a mainstream education on the college level. He was also pleased to have helped hundreds of hearing students learn about Deaf culture and how to communicate in sign language, and he had seen many of them pursue careers related to deafness and deaf people. His role in the founding of NTID meant much to him. "For me," he noted, "It was a growing experience. If I helped others to grow and develop a new awareness of deafness and of the potential of deaf people, so much the better."[5]

The university appreciated the contributions of its first deaf professor. NTID established the Robert F. Panara Scholarship Fund in 1988. He was also awarded the title of professor emeritus. When Paul A. Miller, a former secretary of education for the U.S. government who had served as RIT's sixth president from 1969 to 1979, learned about Bob's retirement, he wrote a very warm note: "You have stood as a giant in our midst. The unfolding of NTID, for which you became a role model, and your wide and considered services to the whole of the Institute, go down in RIT history as among the most exemplary of exploits."[6] NTID's director, William E. Castle, described Bob as "a man whose daily endeavors reflect an untiring sense of dedication and a seemingly limitless imagination."[7]

At the retirement ceremony, the deaf artist and actor Chuck Baird honored Bob by standing before the college's faculty and staff and representing many of Bob's former students with kind words:

I am so happy that I was part of the NTID Drama Club. . . . Bob with his smiling face helped us in many ways not only how to sign a word but with the feeling for the word in a real sense of communication. He put a seed in every one of us to become . . . what we are. . . . All the former and present students and myself wish to express our thanks for the NTID to bring Bob to be our teacher. He taught us to see [that] life [is] beautiful. He has taught us the secret of happiness by giving his example of love for everyone and themselves so we can share that with the world.[8]

Bob had served as NTID's first education specialist, with responsibility for addressing the needs of the deaf college students mainstreamed into the other programs at RIT. That year, Educational Support Service Personnel, an organization serving thirteen states and three provinces in Canada, established the Robert F. Panara Lifetime Achievement Award and announced that he was the first recipient.

His poem "On His Deafness," which had brought him the greatest joy of all the verse he had penned throughout the years, won the $1,000 Grand Prize of the World of Poetry in 1988. The organization honored him as "Golden Poet of the Year" at their national convention in Anaheim, California. Several thousand people, mostly poets from many countries, attended the gathering. Still another highlight of Bob's first year in retirement was the tribute he received from Linda Levitan and former

Bob and Shirley outside the Robert F. Panara Theatre. As NTID's
first deaf faculty member and founder of the Drama Club, Bob was
thrilled to be honored in this way upon retirement from the college.

NTID/RIT student Matthew Moore in *Deaf Life,* including a
cover photograph.

No formal honor, however, pleased Bob more than having
the NTID Theatre named for him. On May 18, 1988, Bill
Castle sent Bob and Shirley an invitation to attend a special
awards ceremony at NTID during the college's National Advisory Group meeting. Castle told Bob that he was delighted to

Bob's former student and cherished friend, Bernard Bragg, returned to NTID numerous times during his career. This visit was during the performance of *Tales of a Clubroom*, which Bragg wrote with Eugene Bergman.

learn that he had won the "Golden Poet" Award from World of Poetry and invited Bob to recite his poem "On His Deafness," at the special ceremony. After a number of awards were announced to various staff and students, Bob stood up and signed his poem. He followed this with his own announcement that he was donating the $1,000 prize to the Robert F. Panara Scholarship Fund. As Bob started to leave the stage with people applauding, Bill Castle motioned for him to stay for a moment. Castle then pulled out a large plaque and held it high with the showmanship he often brought to NTID ceremonies. As Bob stood in shock, Castle announced dramatically, "This plaque commemorates the renaming of the NTID Theatre in honor of Bob. By vote of NTID/RIT, it will henceforth be named the Robert F. Panara Theatre!"

"What a surprise!" Bob recalled. "I was stunned, and could hardly grope for words to express my gratitude. In fact, I was truly 'speechless' for the first time in my professional life."[9] With Shirley wide-eyed and teary, Castle then took her and Bob by the hand and led them to the front of the theater, where a large crowd of people had gathered at a reception in the hall. While people were congratulating Bob, Castle spun him around and said, "Look at the new marquee!" Bob looked up to see the foot-high lettering above the theater entrance: "THE ROBERT F. PANARA THEATRE." This was, according to Bob, the "defining moment of my career, and the best part of it was that Shirley was there to rejoice and share it with me."[10]

As he had done when he left the American School for the Deaf and Gallaudet College, Bob expressed his appreciation for NTID through a poetic tribute.

Making a Pitch

It is no surprise that Bob often connected his passion with baseball and his love for poetry. As Nicholas Dawidoff writes in one of my favorite books, *Baseball: A Literary Anthology*, "Baseball, the most beloved of American sports, is also the most poetic. Its rhythms are those of the seasons. Its memories are savored, its losses lamented."[1] Baseball has also attracted the interest of many American intellectuals. Pulitzer Prize–winner George Will wrote the analytical *Men at Work: The Craft of Baseball*. Presidential historian Doris Kearns Goodwin wrote *Wait Till Next Year: Summer Afternoons with My Father and Baseball*. And *Boston Globe* columnist Tom Oliphant wrote *Praying for Gil Hodges: A Memoir of the 1955 World Series and One Family's Love of the Brooklyn Dodgers*. Ken Burns won an Emmy Award for his documentary miniseries *Baseball*.

Some borrowed lines from Robert Frost's poem "Two Tramps in Mud-Time," express well Bob's pleasure in baseball after his retirement: "My object in living is to unite / My avocation with my vocation / As my two eyes make one in sight." At the ripe age of eighty-nine, Frost, one of the poets often quoted by Bob, also said, "I have never started a poem whose end I knew. Writing the poem is discovering." Pursuing baseball as an avocation in retirement was a discovery for Bob. But he did not stop pursuing poetry, including verse about baseball. Within a year after he retired, he wrote his poem "Field of Dreams."

Bob's avocation is clearly evident in his den at home. He has not one but two large televisions, both of which are always turned on so that he could watch two baseball games simultaneously. The walls of the den are covered with sports memorabilia, reflecting his and Shirley's lifelong love affair with baseball, basketball, football, hockey, and golf. Bob played every one of these sports himself as a young boy in the Bronx. In a place of honor on his wall is an autographed Joe DiMaggio photograph and baseball, Bob's prize possessions. When DiMaggio came to Rochester to sign autographs in 1988, Bob was finally able to meet his idol in person—just for a fleeting moment. Also in his den were *The DiMaggio Albums* sent to him by his sister, Eleanor, in November 1990, which included photos, box scores, and clippings of articles by all the great sports writers of the era. "It was the surprise of a baseball collector's lifetime, and especially of an old Yankee fan," he wrote to Eleanor, "bringing back all those memories of a kid growing up in the Bronx, playing 'hooky' while a student at De Witt Clinton High to pay 50 cents (a week's allowance money) to sit in the bleachers and cheer all my old heroes—DiMaggio, Gehrig, Lazzeri, Gomez, Dickey . . . all the way to Keller, Mantle, and Yogi Berra and Rizzuto."[2]

"There is a marvelous quote by Joe DiMaggio," Bob told me as we sat in his den one evening, "something I always attempted to apply to my teaching. DiMaggio said, 'What I try to do is to keep in mind that everyday there will be a new kid, a kid who has never seen me play before—and I'm going to perform for that kid.'"

This quote is just one of many that show how baseball influenced Bob's teaching. It reminded me of the spring of 1970 at NTID when I first met him and watched him interact with his students. Fresh out of college with no experience in the professional world, I observed him unobtrusively. Every young teacher who wants to be good, I thought, should seek the qualities this man demonstrated. But at the same time, I knew that a rookie would never learn to hit the baseball like Joe DiMaggio, or field a ball like Brooks Robinson, by watching them play. One had to take the bat and glove in hand. As Ralph Waldo Emerson once wrote, "Shakespeare is the only biographer of Shakespeare; and even he can tell nothing, except to the Shakespeare in us; that is, to our most apprehensive and sympathetic hour."[3]

There—I have done it. I have put Shakespeare, baseball, and Emerson all in a single thought about Bob Panara.

But baseball is more than a metaphor and a reality in Bob's life. His avocation became a full-fledged campaign—to induct William Ellsworth "Dummy" Hoy into the National Baseball Hall of Fame. For nearly two decades in his retirement Bob's work toward this end has symbolized, through a baseball motif, his work as a teacher to bring Deaf history to the fore. His classroom was no longer the stage for this advocacy. Now television, newspapers, magazines, and books had become the podium from which he would educate society about what he considered mistreatment of a nineteenth-century deaf baseball player, whose career statistics included stealing 607 bases, scoring 100 runs in a year nine times, and amassing 2,054 hits for a lifetime batting average of .288. Hoy threw out three men at home plate in one game (June 19, 1889), and added another record-breaking feat of a rare 'fielding triple crown' with 45 assists, 337 putouts, and a .977 fielding average in 137 games for the Chicago White Sox in 1900.

Bob began the mainstream movement to promote Hoy for the National Baseball Hall of Fame soon after the publication of his 1983 book *Great Deaf Americans,* which he had co-authored with his son, John.[4] Since then, he had written many letters, making a pitch for Hoy's induction. Now, in retirement, he was able to devote more of his time to this end. In September 1990, he wrote a lengthy letter for the "Speaking Out" page of the *Rochester Democrat and Chronicle* titled "Baseball wouldn't be the same without 'Dummy Hoy.'"[5] Shortly afterwards, he penned a poetic tribute to Hoy, which ran, as he put it in a letter to a friend, "all of 62 lines (one better than Roger Maris). . . . I wanted 'Deaf America' to get excited (and, perhaps, 'up in arms') over the injustice to Hoy."[6] He also sent the *Democrat and Chronicle* article—along with his poem—to the *Silent News,* which published it.[7]

Bob's long poem "William 'Dummy' Hoy" pays tribute to his baseball hero and highlights some of his remarkable feats, as in this excerpt about what a great risk it was for his opponents to try to score from third base to home plate against him:

As on that day of June,
the nineteenth of 1889,
when to the sonic boom
of horsehide smacking mitt
he threw three perfect strikes

from centerfield to the plate
where the catcher, Connie Mack,
stopped each runner in his tracks!
(*The record stands . . .*)

In June of 1989 and with the baseball season underway, Bob was invited by a local televised Deaf talk show *Hey Listen!* to be a guest host on its "Bases Loaded" segment. The show covered a broad range of topics of interest to the Deaf community, and local sports were certainly a focus. The "Bases Loaded" segment featured the Rochester Red Wings manager, Greg Biagini, and the pitching coach, Dick Bosman. Wearing a Red Wings cap and jacket, Bob told anecdotes about "Dummy Hoy" and baseball signs, and interviewed the two Red Wings staff about their own sign systems. After the lively discussion of the ins and outs of modern baseball signs, Bob concluded, "What would baseball be without sign language? It all began with 'Dummy' Hoy, the first deaf player in the major leagues."

One week later, the Rochester Red Wings had a special Deaf Heritage Night. Over four hundred deaf fans turned out. Bob was invited to sign the "Star Spangled Banner" in sign language while standing on the pitcher's mound. He had memorized that song as a child. Confidently, he stood before ten thousand hearing fans, with a friend, Arden Coulston, in the dugout, guiding him regarding the timing. The senior citizen didn't miss a beat. Bob spent his life building bridges from the Deaf world to mainstream culture. While this exposure to the beauty of an ASL version of the "Star Spangled Banner" was a special treat for the fans, Bob had his heart set on completing that one bridge so important to him—the induction of Hoy into the Baseball Hall of Fame. He grabbed every chance he could. On a Saturday evening in August 1992, Bob went to see the Red Wings play the Columbus Clippers. There, he watched the baseball entertainer Max Patkin perform between innings. The "Clown Prince of Baseball" had starred in the movie *Bull Durham,* and Bob was intent on meeting him. After Patkin did his act, Bob went under the stands to the Red Wings' dressing room and knocked on the door (or "rather, pounded" as he put it) until one of the office staff who knew him let him in after he expressed how much he wanted to meet the Clown Prince.

Patkin had just finished dressing and was lacing his shoes. Bob approached Patkin, sat down on the locker room bench beside him, and told him in both speech and sign language how much he enjoyed the Clown Prince's work. After getting Patkin's autograph and even a picture taken together, Bob asked the performer if he had a few minutes. Receiving an affirmative, Bob explained that he had something special in his pocket. He told Patkin that only a week earlier, the man who invented the umpire's signs for strikes and balls—a deaf man named "Dummy" Hoy had been inducted into the Ohio Baseball Hall of Fame. As Bob recalled, "I expected him to show a casual interest. . . . But not Max Patkin. He showed a genuine interest in the . . . [Ohio Hall of Fame] Brochure."[8]

Bob stalked everyone he could find to support the campaign for Hoy. It would not, however, be an exaggeration to claim that baseball, at times, stalked Bob, too. He looked a lot like Joe Altobelli, "Mr. Red Wings," and he was occasionally mistaken for the former manager while walking through Silver Stadium, the home of that team. One evening, when we were walking near the souvenir store, a group of kids asked Bob for his autograph. "Sorry to disappoint you," he told them. "I'm just a fan, like you." One of the kids, about ten years old, kept trailing Bob and poking a pencil and the game program in his stomach. Bob smiled, pulled out his wallet, and showed the kid his driver's license photograph. "Now, do you believe me?" The kid frowned and with a puzzled expression walked off with his friends.

As Bob worked in the grassroots movement sponsored by the American Athletic Association of the Deaf, the "William 'Dummy' Hoy Committee" with Randy Fisher as chairman, he and the other members also aimed at increasing public awareness of Hoy's achievements. In 1992 Bob attended Hoy's induction to the Hall of Fame in Maumee, Ohio, establishing a friendship with the then president, Thomas C. Eakin, who had transformed "The Cy Young Museum" into the Ohio Baseball Hall of Fame. Bob sent out an article about Hoy's induction to numerous publications in the field of deafness and wrote to Eakin thanking him again for his efforts. Regretfully, he added, "Aside from that nice write up—with photos—that appeared in *The Toledo Blade* [August 14, 1992], I have yet to see anything in the press about 'Dummy Hoy' being inducted." He then expressed hope that that would happen in due time. "And I am sure that, somewhere up in the wide blue yonder, Dummy Hoy is smiling and basking in the eternal sunlight with the knowledge that he has not been forgotten!"[9]

Shirley strongly supported Bob's every effort to promote Hoy. Meeting the couple in local restaurants in Rochester was always a fascinating experience. For years, they had made their rounds, "working the room." They were on a first-name basis with many table servers and managers. Shirley had taught the staff signs during their meals in some places. They talked about families and sports, swapped photographs of grandchildren, and generally spread good cheer wherever they went. Because of Rochester's unusually large deaf population—about fifty thousand deaf and hard-of-hearing people—it is easy for a deaf couple to "fit." Shirley also taught sign language to elderly ladies in the community who were losing their hearing. No matter where they went—the post office, gas stations, food markets, or parks—the Panaras were well known. They both corresponded continually with friends and former students, not only via letters and e-mail, but also exchanging "video letters" with Ernest Marshall, the pioneer in deaf motion picture films.

It was during their many walks near their home one afternoon that Bob and Shirley noticed a friendly neighbor's dog, King Pup, a midsize terrier, chained to a long leash and pining away in his backyard. King Pup belonged to a family in which both the husband and wife worked full-time and their teenaged kids were never home. When Bob and Shirley asked the Granville family if they could take King Pup for walks when nobody was home, they were delighted. They were planning to give him away to a nice family, and they believed King Pup could not go to a better one.

Bob's colleagues at NTID had given him a new set of golf clubs for use in his retirement. Shirley loved golf. She first took the sport up after she and Bob married, and they had played together while living in Maryland. A nearby golf course was often the site of celebrity tourneys, and as the fledgling LPGA got off to a shaky start, Shirley met such greats as Babe Didrikson Zaharias, Marlene Hagge, Patty Berg, and other star players. After the Panaras moved to Rochester in 1967, Shirley continued to play golf, as time and her work permitted. Then, in 1978, Rochester started hosting the LPGA Tournament at Locust Hill Country Club not far from their home. Shirley was overjoyed. Over the years, Shirley and champion golfer Nancy Lopez became friends, and during the annual LPGA tournaments in Rochester, Shirley and Bob would push forward to the front of the crowds. When the pros passed by, Shirley would yell out their names. "Nancy! Nancy!" she shouted one afternoon, as fans nearby doubtlessly wondered what was going on. Recognizing Shirley's distinctive speech, Nancy Lopez came over and gave her a hug. Over the years, Shirley got to know such great players as Patty Sheehan, Julie Inkster, Betsy King, and Joanne Carner—all Hall of Famers. She took a special liking to rising star Wendy Ward, who, in appreciation, surprised Shirley on her seventy-ninth birthday, June 23, 2002, with a golf visor bearing thirty-seven autographs of the LPGA contestants.

Shirley was to golf what Bob was to baseball. But she loved a baseball game as well. Sometimes in the spring they would visit about a half dozen training camps in Florida to see some games before the season began. Babysitting Erin and Billy kept the retired couple both spry and active. On Bob and Shirley's birthdays, John and his family treated them to cookouts at their home, followed by softball in their backyard. John continued another family tradition. He became the coach of Erin's Little League team as well as of Billy's Pony League team. "Lots of excitement," the proud grandfather wrote to his sister, Eleanor, and her husband John. "Last week, Erin's team upset the undefeated league leaders, and this week Bill's team beat the No. 1 and No. 2 teams in his league. So the coach must be doing something good!"[10]

Brooks Robinson had been Bob's favorite living ballplayer since the 1960s. The Panaras saw the incomparable "Human Vacuum Cleaner" play third base for the Orioles countless times in Washington, D.C., and Baltimore. Years earlier, Bob had the opportunity to meet Robinson, and he was pleasantly surprised that the Oriole knew how to fingerspell fluently. Robinson had been born and raised in Little Rock, Arkansas, and used to play against the team from the nearby school for the deaf. Bob also met Robinson several times during spring training in Florida. After Bob retired from NTID, Robinson came to Rochester for an autograph-signing session. Bob showed him some photos he had taken at a past meeting and got a delightful reaction:

> He lights up . . . remembers "the deaf guy" and starts finger-spelling to the astonishment of everybody lined up and stand-ing around . . . we had a nice talk after he finished signing . . . [he] actually signed eight . . . items—photos, books, balls—for me and my grandkids . . . Swell guy, Brooks—affable, easy-going, warmhearted—the best.[11]

Bob also got Brooks Robinson to endorse Hoy for the Hall of Fame, and be an ex officio member of the Hoy Committee.

As the battle for Hoy's induction went on and on, Bob was disappointed repeatedly. On February 27, 1996, Eakin formally submitted Hoy's name for election to the Veterans Committee of the National Baseball Hall of Fame in Cooperstown. He wrote that Sam Crawford, a Hall of Famer, had said that Hoy was responsible for plate umpires giving hand signals to call balls [and] strikes, and that "'Dummy' Hoy's enshrinement in the National Baseball Hall of Fame would be cherished by all baseball fans."[12] Thus, by 1996, Bob and his group had succeeded in getting Hoy on the Cooperstown annual ballot twice, but as he wrote to Scott Pitoniak, sportswriter for the *Rochester Democrat and Chronicle* newspaper, "We have been shut out in the final voting."[13]

The following year, 1997, Pitoniak described Bob's battle in the *Democrat and Chronicle* as one that was "passionately and eloquently" fought on Hoy's behalf.[14] In the spring of 1998, Pitoniak wrote to him that he was sorry to see that the Veterans Committee again overlooked Hoy. "But you can't give up the fight," Pitoniak encouraged.[15] More troubling to Bob was the fact that the Hall of Fame Veterans Committee, composed of a group of former players and baseball executives responsible for considering candidates from the nineteenth century, used a secret ballot, which hides the identity of players being considered.[16] As Matt Leingang reported in the *Democrat and Chronicle* in February 2000 in another front-page story about Bob, titled "Going to bat for a deaf hero," many observers of the Hall of Fame induction process have said that the Veterans Committee "is reluctant to vote for old-timers they never saw perform."[17] For that reason, Leingang wrote, nineteenth-century players like Hoy are truly disadvantaged.[18]

Bob continued to fight for recognition of this deaf baseball player. His contacts included Darryl Brock, who was writing the fact-based fictional novel, *Havana Heat,* about another deaf baseball player, "Dummy Taylor." The Hoy Committee, with hundreds of deaf and hearing fans, boldly lobbied for their cause at the Induction Day ceremony in Cooperstown on August 3, 1997. Linda Levitan wrote a summary of the event in *Deaf Life* magazine titled "So near, yet so far: rallying for "Dummy" Hoy in Cooperstown." But the rally was to no avail.

Hall of Famer Rogers Hornsby once said, "People ask me what I do in winter when there's no baseball. I'll tell you what I do. I stare out the window and wait for spring." Bob wasn't like that. Between baseball seasons, he never remained idle. An avid Buffalo Bills fan, in the early 1990s, three generations of Panaras—Bob, John, and teenage Bill—had season seats when the Buffalo Bills had their dynasty. They saw the three home championship games and they were there when the Bills achieved the greatest comeback in NFL history, storming back from a 35-to-3 deficit to beat the Houston Oilers, 41 to 38 in overtime in a 1993 playoff game. Like typical Bills fans, they would always arrive early before the game and enjoy a bit of "tailgating" in the parking lot. Their ritual included throwing a football around. John remembered one afternoon, when his father made a sparkling catch right in front of a group of rowdy young tailgaters. They all applauded and gave the retired deaf professor "high fives."

In 2003, twenty years after the campaign began, there was still little promise that Hoy would ever be inducted. I remember the day when Bob gave me a copy of Stephen Jay Gould's book *Triumph and Tragedy in Mudville: A Lifelong Passion for Baseball.* Bob was excited to see that the distinguished writer and anthropologist Stephen Jay Gould had gotten into the battle in support of Dummy Hoy. In the chapter on Dummy Hoy, Gould mentions Bob's writing about his hero. Bob could not agree more with Gould's final paragraph:

> Let us therefore enshrine Dummy Hoy for whatever eternity means in baseball. Only then will we break the circle of silence that still surrounds this intelligent, savvy, wonderfully skilled, and exemplary man who also happened to be deaf, while giving his life to a sport never well played by ear.[19]

Each of Bob's deaf friends had baseball heroes, but we all harbored that dream of Hoy's induction as well. My own hero was Roberto Clemente. I had grown up in Pittsburgh. On one memorable baseball evening with Bob, June 2, 1995, at the old Silver Stadium, the seventh-inning stretch brought the fans to their feet to sing "Take Me Out to the Ballgame." As Bob was wont to do, he signed along with the words on the scoreboard, everyone around him enjoying his dramatic rendition. As a season ticket holder, Bob had established his own personal fiefdom at the stadium, and throughout the game there was an endless line of his own fans stopping by to see him—former students and colleagues, ushers, Ogden Whitehead, the deaf cheerleading stadium staff member who, with his colorful uniform, was popular among the kids and adults alike, Red Wings president Gary Larder, and other officials from the team. They all gravitated to Bob as if he were a baseball celebrity himself. He was one of the most likable and supportive fans in the history of that farm team.

At this particular game, Bob had planned everything carefully to be *my* evening. As the singing stopped, he nudged my arm with his elbow and pointed at the scoreboard situated across the field from where we were sitting. I looked up to see the words flashing on the screen for the entire stadium to read: "HAPPY BIRTHDAY, HARRY LANG, FROM YOUR BUDDY BOB PANARA!"

Bob handed me a copy of the game program and pointed at a page inside where the same birthday message was printed. He had planned this surprise, too, with the ballpark staff. Nor was the evening over when the game ended. Following such outings, it was typical for us to sit in his driveway and talk for an hour

Harry Lang and Bob Panara enjoying a Red Wings game.

about the game and our plans to spend time together during the next few weeks. This time, however, Shirley saw us in the driveway and came out to take our picture together as Bob handed me a birthday gift I would never forget—a biography of my childhood hero, Pittsburgh Pirate Roberto Clemente, who was killed in an airplane crash while delivering relief supplies and food to Nicaragua following the devastation of an earthquake. Like many other youngsters growing up in Pittsburgh, I had plastered Clemente's pictures all over my bedroom walls. A hundred of my own childhood baseball memories flashed through my mind that evening as I thanked Bob for the gift book.

Bob was just as familiar with the baseball passions of his other friends and his son. When John was twelve years old, he had been fortunate enough to have his picture taken with idol Brooks Robinson during training camp in Fort Lauderdale. Bob later surprised him with an enlargement, personally autographed by Brooks. Over the years, I saw Bob give unique presents to other friends who shared nearby seats. Ed Maruggi got a book on Italian baseball players. Sal Parlato got a baseball autographed by Joe Altobelli, the former Baltimore Orioles manager who managed the Rochester Red Wings for six seasons and took them to two Governor's Cups (Championships of the International League). Among his gifts to his daughter-in-law Janis, an avid Yankee fan, was an autographed baseball card of the Yankees' Derek Jeter. Almost the entire section surrounding Bob's reserved seats had become like a happy family. Nick Christakis, the section usher, would often bring family pictures to show his deaf friend. Directly in front of Bob's seat sat the baseball savant Steve Shencup, who was Bob's equal in baseball trivia. Next to Steve sat Lynne Ginnane, who surprised Bob on his eighty-sixth birthday by bringing a large chocolate cake to a baseball game.

By 2006, after several decades of making the pitch for the induction of Dummy Hoy into the Baseball Hall of Fame at Cooperstown, Bob's baseball hero had still not received the recognition he deserved. But on July 15 that year, Bob realized another dream. On that date, the Massachusetts Mutual Life Insurance Company, in cooperation with *Exceptional Parent Magazine* and the Rochester Red Wings, sponsored "Disability Awareness Night" at Frontier Field, honoring contributions made by, and on behalf of, fifty-four million Americans with disabilities. Bob was asked to receive the award for NTID. Over the forty years since Bob began teaching at the college, thousands of highly qualified deaf graduates had entered professions that previously had not been open to them. With his son, John, as his colleague and interpreter, Bob marched to the mound, where the Red Wings' general manager Dan Mason announced to a full stadium that not only was Bob the first deaf professor at NTID, and that the theater, which has become a Rochester landmark in theatrical performances, was named for him, but that he was also one of the biggest Red Wings fans in the stadium. "Then, with my son watching, came the 'defining moment on *my* field of dreams,'" Bob e-mailed me while I was out of town. "I was handed a ball on that sacred spot—where I had often dreamed of standing—to throw out the first pitch!"

Rustle of a Star

Bob's fight for Hoy's induction was just one of many projects in retirement. He never intended that "retirement" would mean "leisure." "I wonder if I'll get to see as much of Shirley, and the country, as we hoped by retiring," he wrote to Ralph Hoag, former superintendent of the Rochester School for the Deaf. It seemed that he only "retired" at bedtime each evening.[1]

Among his many pursuits, he built on his pioneering work in Deaf Studies through writing. In 1989 I invited him to co-author an analysis of "Deaf People and Deafness in Science Fiction." That year he proved that there was still magic in those hands when he enthralled a group of deaf high school students during a "Poet-in-Residence" week at my alma mater, the Western Pennsylvania School for the Deaf (WPSD) in Pittsburgh. There he illustrated start-up methods for short poems and explained the function of poetic imagery and figures of speech. His discussion of the last stanza of British poet William Ernest Henley's "Invictus," demonstrated his unique ability to enhance student understanding of poetic imagery and was captured in a videotaped documentary.[2] As Bob had done with many other students during his career as a teacher, he not only imparted

"Be the poem" was Bob Panara's approach to teaching. In this photograph, Bob asks a deaf high school student to act out his own poem at the Western Pennsylvania School for the Deaf in 1989.

knowledge, he also empowered the twelfth-graders to interpret the meaning of the words they were reading. On this particular afternoon, the young men and women, who had never met a deaf poet before, examined the following four lines: "It matters not how strait the gate, / How charged with punishments the scroll, / I am the master of my fate: / I am the captain of my soul." Bob led them far beyond interpreting the meaning of terms. They were translating the meaning of the poem in terms of their own lives. One could see in their faces the growing comprehension of—and appreciation for—poetry. That was Bob's goal—to teach these students to love language, whether in print or in sign. They discussed the notion of being "invincible." They gave him examples from history. The discussion of Henley's verse was time well spent. These students left the classroom knowing what was meant by being a "captain of my soul." They had just spent an hour reflecting on their own character, aspirations, and beliefs.

In a class of seventh-graders in this school, he encouraged the deaf students to analyze the poem "Dreams" by the African American poet Langston Hughes. "What things in the poem are related to the title?" he asked. "What is the big idea of the poem?" "Why is it important to hold on to your dreams?" He encouraged each of these young deaf students to discover, express, and hold onto *their* dreams, conquering all obstacles including the communication and attitude barriers they faced.

Bob also worked with younger hearing children. His granddaughter, Erin, recalls how he inspired her fourth-grade class of hearing children when he came for a guest presentation on poetry while she was student teaching. "I observed how much the students were engaged and captivated by the presentation. In their eyes I could see excitement and true interest in what my grandfather was doing. . . . Weeks after my grandfather had left, students continued to recite his poems and practice sign language!"[3]

Over the next few years, Bob assisted Jane Maher, an English professor at Nassau Community College on Long Island, who was writing her dissertation on the work of William Stokoe. Maher had Stokoe's permission and planned to have the dissertation published. Bob shared his perspectives on the Gallaudet experience and wished her the best with her work. Maher's work culminated in the book *Seeing Language in Sign: The Work of William C. Stokoe*. In 1996 Bob collaborated with Matthew Moore in a revised and updated edition of *Great Deaf*

Americans. In a moment of nostalgia, he also wrote "Idylls of the Green" for a book published by the National Association of the Deaf, *Deafness: Historical Perspectives*. In seven stanzas of poetry, he captured more about his student days at college than he could have done in seventy pages of prose. The poem struck a nerve among many fellow graduates, who flooded Bob with complimentary letters. Old friends sent him personal notes about how he so vividly captured life on Kendall Green in that storied "Victorian" era.

Bob long expressed hope to his friends that he could publish his "little sonatas" along with other selected poems he had written. "Shirley has been on my neck for years, begging me to publish such a collection," he wrote to fellow poet Rex Lowman two years before he retired. "I realize that poetry doesn't sell nowadays—but it would be worth [it to me] to

Shirley and Bob celebrated fifty years of marriage in 1997.

produce a 'labor amoris.' *That* is a promise I made to Shirley on Labor Day!"[4] This promise became even more important to him in retirement. Shirley was battling lymphoma. Several of his poems had been devoted to her, and he had his heart on seeing them printed in a volume of his verse. He wrote to his sister, Eleanor, about Shirley's cancer: "Nothing ever makes her spirit droop."[5] Shortly afterwards, John and Janis surprised Bob and Shirley with a fiftieth-wedding-anniversary dinner party at a picturesque Erie Canal restaurant.

Bob's dream of publication was culminated when Deaf Life Productions brought out a collection of his personal poetry. *On His Deafness and Other Melodies Unheard* is a collection of sixty-six poems and two essays and was published on the occasion of Bob's seventy-fifth birthday. It gathered in one place the popular "On His Deafness," along with his witty college verse, the touching war poems, his tributes to respected contemporaries, poetic glimpses at his beloved world of baseball, and his romantic verses.

In 1998 Bob received the RIT Founders Award at NTID's Thirtieth Anniversary Academic Convocation, when NTID's first deaf dean, T. Alan Hurwitz, was installed. I. King Jordan, Gallaudet University's first deaf president, wrote him, "You are a giant in the field and highly deserving of all the honors and awards that come your way and many more."[6] In 1999, Bob was chosen as Educator of the Quarter Century by *Silent News,* the major news periodical of the American deaf community. Bob was again delighted when his signature poem was published in an anthology edited by the distinguished writer Robert DiYanni. Mary DiYanni, Robert's niece and a teacher at the

Fanwood school in White Plains, had read Bob's book of verse. She rushed home to show her uncle. DiYanni was so impressed with "On His Deafness" that he asked Bob for permission to include it in his forthcoming edition of *Literature: Fiction, Poetry, Drama, and the Essay.* "Imagine!" Bob told me, "I was featured alongside of Shelley and Byron, T. S. Eliot and Frost, and Sophocles and Shakespeare!"[7]

One of the most entertaining characteristics of Bob's correspondence with his friends is the manner in which he peppers his informal writing with Shakespeare. "That's all 'for the nonce,'" is a frequent closing in his e-mail notes to me, a Shakespearean corruption of "for then once" (*King Henry VI*). "I can no other answer make but thanks, / And thanks, and ever thanks" (*Twelfth Night*), he wrote to RIT's provost, Stan McKenzie, who sent him kind words at his retirement. He fondly remembers Mr. Ferber from De Witt Clinton High School, who had encouraged him to recite his first passage from Shakespeare, a soliloquy from *Macbeth.* And during the 1980s, when American Sign Language was quickly developing as a form of visual expression, he published an article in which he quoted from Shakespeare's *Hamlet* on how ASL "suits the action to the word."[8]

In retirement, Bob often walked King Pup in Mendon Ponds Park, "sort of like Thoreau's 'Walden,'" he wrote to his friend George Propp, "where I recite poetry and Shakespearean monologues aloud while in marching time. King Pup must have the best background in literary studies of a canine."[9] In later life, Bob explained, he was always able to bring back any lyric poem or poetic prose passage he had taught in his classes over the years. "They enabled me to enjoy those hours spent in solitude, or to quote at will poetry, Shakespearean passages."

Many of Bob's former students carried on his love for Shakespeare. As Willy Conley, a deaf playwright who has become chairman of the theater department at Gallaudet University, reflected, "I have acted professionally in four Shakespeare productions to date; I don't think I would have ever been involved if I had not received the access and strength to immerse myself in Shakespeare from Bob." By "access," Willy explained, "Shakespeare was quite inaccessible for me until Bob enacted famous passages in dramatic ASL in the classroom."[10]

When interviewed about his career as a teacher by John Clark for *The Tactile Mind* in 2003, Bob was asked which "works of art . . . grace the most treasured part of your pleasure?"[11] Shakespeare's plays were at the top of his list. His students carried on the enthusiasm about Shakespeare to their own families. Former NTID student Jeanne Behm wrote, "Through ASL, Panara ignited my love for Shakespeare and poetry during my college days. He gave me tools or ways to dramatize or express written language in my public speaking opportunities today. What I have learned from him, I passed on to my children when I home-schooled them. Panara has been my inspiration that I will treasure."[12]

Even people Bob had never met were touched by his passion for Shakespeare. In December 1987 Noreen Collins wrote to him, "I wanted to let you know about your influence on me many years ago. In 1974, you came to speak at Mill Neck

School for the Deaf on Long Island, NY, for graduation. I was the English teacher in the high school at that time, having just graduated with a B.S. in Deaf Education the year previous. You inspired me with your talk of Shakespeare for my deaf students, and you helped me see that there's more to language than just English! . . . No matter what the language, verbal or non-verbal, the import I give to it is due to your influence. I just wanted to say thank you!"[13]

In January 2001, my wife, Bonnie Meath-Lang, artistic director in NTID's performing arts program, conceived and directed a theatrical tribute to Bob that highlighted his passion for both literature and baseball. As the theater program discussed its twenty-fifth season the previous May, the faculty and artists felt that it was time to reconnect a new generation of students to the importance of Bob's work and the establishment of the theater in which they were performing. By that time, ninety-three NTID performing arts students had worked in some form of professional theater, and many more had become leaders in the Deaf community.

The performance, "The Rustle of a Star: A Tribute to the Life and Art of Robert F. Panara," took the form of a fantasy based on the literary and historical influences on his life, exploring the incalculable influence of a master teacher. It was written to honor him on his eightieth birthday.

The premise of the play is a dream by a student/muse figure, whose reading touches on the themes and characters connected to Bob. In this "other dimension" of the student's reverie, there is a chance encounter between Will Shakespeare and Dummy Hoy, who, while other characters appear inexplicably, try to find their connection.

Bob loved the clever tribute Bonnie had developed. He wrote to his old college friend, Malz, describing the play:

> Along comes Juliet and other assorted characters who do their bit to entertain the two Wills with poetry, song, and dance from Literature, Art, and Drama—all the while with the Bard and Hoy still trying to figure out why they had been brought together. Enter Cleopatra, Kate (of "The Shrew") and Portia (the wise), who after some clever deduction involving names, places, and things, come up with the solution: There is a man in the audience who helped to found NTID, the Theatre Program, the English Department, the Theatre which is named for him, and has written about and actively campaigned to get Hoy in the Hall of Fame.[14]

During the curtain call, the two actors who had played Macbeth and Macduff saluted Bob with their swords, and the cast called him and Shirley onto the stage to honor him at the last performance.

Shirley was also feted in this play, in a monologue titled "Shirley Valentine" by the Deaf professional actor Mary Vreeland. Their son, John, was one of the actors, voicing for the signing of Bob's poem "On His Deafness" and for Costello in the "Who's on First?" skit.

With the naming of the theater after him years earlier, the sign-name PANARA had lived on within the NTID building. The students who had never met Bob were thrilled over his attendance at each performance—and the cast parties. One student remarked to Bonnie, "I never had grandparents who could communicate with me. After all those evenings talking to and listening to the Panaras and their stories, I feel like I've adopted some smart, cool grandparents!"

Heart and Soul

For more than three decades, I have been teaching a methods course for aspiring teachers in the NTID Master of Science in Secondary Education program. For many of those years there was little research to guide us. What should be emphasized in such a course? In 1990, as part of the Teaching Research Program in the NTID Department of Educational Research and Teacher Education, I surveyed more than a hundred teachers to identify their priorities. The top three areas mentioned were first, the characteristics of effective teachers; second, teaching styles that work best with deaf learners; and finally, aspects of effective communication in the classroom. We conducted a number of studies and found that, like hearing students, deaf students highly value a teacher's knowledge of the *content*. They also value teachers who are caring, establish rapport with them, sign clearly, and demonstrate their enjoyment of teaching. Bob Panara was a prime example of a master teacher who had developed these and other important characteristics through intuition and experience.

Bob incorporated into his teaching style many concepts we value today. He was a social constructivist long before that theory became popular. He believed that learning should be an interactive experience. It was critical that his students bring their own experiences into the discussions. In discussing his Deaf Studies course, he emphasized the importance of student-centeredness: "a student reading a short story, novel, or play [should] compare his own deaf experience with the experience of that deaf character in the literary work; and show whether it is true or false, add something of his own experience that parallels that, and maybe try to show how it symbolizes the experience of Everyman also."[1] Similarly, the empowerment he promoted through his teaching reflects Paulo Freire's critical pedagogy; the self-confidence he developed in his students, further evidenced by their success upon graduation, is the hallmark of Albert Bandura's work.

During all his years growing up, Bob's son, John, told me one afternoon, he never once heard his father speak negatively about a student or a student's writing. "His heart just wouldn't let him do such a thing." John remembers an article written by Alex Haley, in which he advised, "Find the good—and praise it."[2] When it came to his deaf students, Bob always found a way to do just that. Alan Gifford, a deaf civil engineer who took several courses with Bob in integrated classes with both deaf and hearing students at RIT, remembered that it was always fun to watch the students being mesmerized by Bob's style of teaching. "He never put anyone down. His impact on me was that he helped me to understand my deaf heritage in a way, which provided me the necessary tools to be assertive in society. He helped me and many others to accept deafness as our silent partner as it is always with us no matter where we go."[3] Alan attributed this attitude instilled in him in Bob's course to his success as a construction manager and elected official in the community.

Throughout the first year after Shirley had invited me to write his biography, Bob and I had many discussions about how his life influenced his teaching. When baseball season ended in the fall of 2002, we would go to hockey games. The Rochester Americans, an American Hockey League team, were always entertaining. After the games I often had a few questions to discuss with him. With every story he told about his life, I felt our friendship grow stronger. Through the holidays and into the spring, I continued to collect many reminiscences of his family's heritage, his childhood, and his experiences as a teacher. Shirley, too, had had a fulfilling life. Her independent work as a cataloguer at the Library of Congress and as a librarian at the White Plains School for the Deaf and Rochester School for the Deaf, had led to her own legacy of students who remembered her for inspiring them with a passion for books. She had always enjoyed interacting with the celebrities as well. She was a good friend with Nanette Fabray, who served on NTID's National Advisory Group for a few years, and when the Panaras picked her up at the airport, they would sometimes take her to their home to rest and chat. They had gotten to know Fabray while living in California. Shirley was also close friends with Frances Woods of "The Wonder Dancers" fame (with Billy Bray), and closely followed their career. After a private tour of NTID with Jane Fonda, Shirley had an intimate chat with the movie star about her father, Henry, who was at the time suffering from poor health. The stories made the visits to the Panara home a great joy. Bob's son, John, was also a key source of information. Even after he had become a teacher of deaf students at NTID himself, there were moments when he was reminded why his father was revered as a master teacher. He recalled one afternoon when he met his mom and dad for lunch. He had taught a couple of classes that morning and recounted what had happened:

> As a matter of fact, I was feeling pretty clever. I explained to my parents how I had introduced the concept of "outlining" to the class by associating the sign for "skeleton" with it, my point being that an outline is more like the bare bones of a composition—something to give the reader a general picture of what will be in the essay. I mentioned how I had told the class to start with the bare bones and then work on adding the meat later. Made perfect sense, right? However, I still vividly recall my father's comment after I had given my little narrative at the restaurant. Dad looked me straight in the eye and said, "Bones . . . meat . . . okay, but what about the *heart*?"[4]

It should be no surprise to anyone who knows Bob that one of his favorite songs is "You Gotta Have Heart," from the hit Broadway musical *Damn Yankees*. As the lyrics go: "All you really need is heart / When the odds are sayin' you'll never win / That's when the grin should start." Bob actually once formed a duet with his deaf friend Mac Norwood and signed this song onstage at a National Association of the Deaf banquet in Washington, D.C. He had gone to Griffith Stadium and asked Calvin Griffith, the owner of the Senators, if he could borrow two Senators' uniforms. Griffith grinned at Bob, "Anything to beat the Damn Yankees!"[5]

As John told me, this sums up a lot about his father, about his philosophy and why he was such a great teacher-performer. Imagining baseball players dancing in their uniforms and singing for a team that's "gotta have heart" is not much different from Bob's technique of drawing "pictures in the air" with his hands in the classroom. No matter what obstacles he encountered, he kept his heart.

Teaching from the heart meant teaching with meaning, motivating students, and involving them in ways that would instill a love for learning. Four lines of his classic poem "On His Deafness," tie together his love for language and for teaching: "For I have learned from Fancy's artisan / How written words can thrill the inner ear / Just as they move the heart, and so for me / They also seem to ring out loud and free."

Teaching from the "soul," on the other hand, clearly had its roots in Ralph Waldo Emerson. John proudly referred to his dad as a Transcendentalist. This is a characteristic many of Bob's colleagues might not necessarily pick up on by watching Bob's teaching alone. This intimate side of Bob's teaching is found in his unpublished correspondence, his master's thesis, and his course notes from decades ago. These materials enrich our understanding of this man. His published lectures, journal articles, books, and even his verse are often pragmatic, and one must dig deeper to find the "soul" of his teaching. He enjoyed drawing parallels with himself and the more famous Transcendentalists. To newspaper writer Greg Livadas, Bob once said, "It's nice to be shut off from the sound and fury of this stupid world and enjoy total silence like Thoreau could enjoy whenever he walked in his Walden Pond."[6] Throughout the seven decades since he became deaf, Bob has taken advantage of the silence in his own world to find the "inner revelation," which, in his own words to his students in 1955, "gives every moment in his life tremendous significance."[7]

For Bob, teaching from the soul was also a process of fostering wonder, freeing oneself as far as possible of external pressures and politics and recognizing the dignity of the classroom. It is poetry, or as Shelley once said, something that "lifts the veil from the hidden beauty of the world, and makes familiar objects be as if they were not familiar." It is empowerment, not only of students, but also of oneself. It is knowing—and believing—that teachers can make a difference; it is searching for meaning and sharing what we have learned with others who teach. In Bob's own verse, "Poets and Poetry":

Ah, if they knew the poet has a soul!
Like cheering schoolboys catching a parade,
He, too, must follow where the caissons roll,
For as the pulses sing the song is made.
So, seek him not within a gilded cage
But feel him rubbing elbows with the age!

I stopped over to see Bob one evening to chat about this notion of his being "transcendental" as a teacher. It fascinated me to see how he had absorbed Transcendentalism without making a conscious effort. I was impressed by how Bob, as a deaf person, had focused on the sense of *vision* in transcendence. As a scientist, I was particularly interested in how he had examined some lines of an Emerson poem: "these young scholars who invade our hills / Love not the flower they pluck and know it not / And all their botany is Latin names." In 1956 Bob had published a paper on Santayana's "sense of beauty," in which he wrote, "It would appear to me as though both Santayana, the philosopher, and Emerson, the poet-seer, are in accord relative to the probability that, in the final analysis, the eye transcends both reason and feeling in the perception of Beauty."[8]

While searching for how Bob translated the beauty of things in his verse through visual perception, I had accidentally spilled coffee on my copy of his book of poems *On His Deafness—and Other Melodies Unheard,* and Bob had promised me a new copy. When I arrived at his house, he was in his T-shirt, having just awakened from a nap. His kitchen table, as always, was strewn with piles of letters, cards, and magazines. A lifetime of building friendships kept him busy with correspondence in retirement. He would often share letters with me from his former students. Over the next year I interviewed many of them. But I was especially pleased that the RIT library had kept many tapes from his classes at NTID. I also found some from his Gallaudet years. These tapes supported what his students shared with me. They supported his stories of the influence of his former teachers and validated how his adventures in self-directed learning in mainstream classes when he was young had become part of his repertoire of knowledge and skills. In sum, his life experiences were there on tape in the form of his instruction.

My focus on the "heart and soul" in Bob's teaching was going well as we also enjoyed baseball outings and continued to chat with Shirley about their past. Our discussions revealed the tremendous influence this woman had exerted on Bob's life, his teaching, and his writings. Then tragedy struck.

Bob was celebrating his birthday on July 8, 2003, at home with Shirley. They had brought sandwiches to the family room and looked forward to watching the televised Ladies Professional Golf Association playoffs. They were all set to watch the tournament when Bob glanced over to get Shirley's attention. She did not respond. Her eyes were half shut and her arms were hanging limp. Bob immediately dialed 911, and the ambulance arrived within ten minutes. They checked Shirley's breathing and blood pressure, and much to Bob's relief, she showed signs of alertness, and she was able to move her arms. He nevertheless took her to Highland Hospital Emergency Room.

Shirley seemed to recover fairly quickly. On July 10, Bob sent me a cheerful note: "Things are looking good, thank God!" There were no obvious aftereffects other than her feeling tired. Bob had exhausted himself going back and forth to the hospital. "You'll have to wait another week," he joked, "before receiving any more stuff from this 'paragraph factory.'"[9]

Over the few days following this episode, both the family doctor and a specialist checked on Shirley each morning. They gave her CAT scans, sonar echograms, and MRIs. "She now is just about normal," Bob e-mailed me. "She is up and walking; talks and signs as usual." The doctors first diagnosed the problem as a case of atrial fibrillation (a "floppy valve" in the lower left chamber), and they put Shirley on blood thinners and anticoagulants to prevent blood clots. Bob e-mailed me the good news: "The doctor said she can return home tomorrow!"[10]

Then at home on Saturday, July 12, their wedding anniversary, Shirley began experiencing intense pain, this time a result of bleeding in the stomach from an overdose of blood thinners. Bob rushed her to the hospital again. On Sunday morning, Shirley fell into a coma. I rushed to the hospital and stayed the day with Bob. We both sensed what was ahead. Unspoken, unsigned thoughts filled the silence for what seemed like hours. We sat in that gloomy hospital room watching over Shirley . . . and hoping.

Meanwhile, Bonnie had left an urgent answering machine message for John and his family, who were returning from Toronto that day. After arriving home and hearing the message, they immediately raced to the hospital. We all shared in the grief as Bob signed the form to permit the doctor to take Shirley off the oxygen. Nothing could be done. John stayed through the night with his mother while Bob went home to get some sleep.

For the next few days Shirley remained in a coma. We took turns supporting Bob through the final days of Shirley's life. On Wednesday morning, July 16, 2003, Bob's beloved wife passed away. I have tried to find the right words to describe Bob's emotions on this day, and there seem to be no better words to express their long marriage than those of the Austrian drama-tist Friedrich Halm: "Two souls with but a single thought, Two hearts that beat as one."[11]

Grandson Bill was with Bob and my wife Bonnie the mo-ment Shirley passed away. Bill remembered how touched he was when Bob took Shirley's hands and said: "These hands are so precious; I can remember all the things you did with them— teaching me to drive, giving baby Johnny a bath in the kitchen sink of our first apartment, doing all the beds, laundry, cook-ing meals, hosting parties, telling stories in the libraries to deaf children, catching baseballs with Johnny, and then later with Bill and Erin."[12]

At the wake the following week, hundreds of deaf and hear-ing friends came to pay their respects. Former students, neigh-bors, colleagues who had worked with Bob for twenty years at

NTID, friends from other states, waitresses from local restaurants, staff from the Henrietta Town Post Office—these and many more waited in line to comfort Bob. Among the floral tributes delivered to the funeral home was a beautiful bouquet from the Rochester Red Wings baseball team.

On one table stood a photograph of Shirley. Her words to Bob written fifty-six years ago echo in my memory, "Darling, I will love you always, with the fondest of memories." On a card attached to a personal bouquet, Bob had written the very same words.

One night shortly after the wake, as Bob sat at home with King Pup by his side, he thought about Shirley's many hobbies, including collecting pairs of animals for a model of Noah's Ark, which she kept on a shelf in the family room. The sonnet he wrote in Shirley's memory is touched by grief.

Two by Two
There was a time I used to wonder why
Your heart went out to creatures great and small,
Like "Noah's Ark," you made them multiply
With mini look alikes bought at the Mall.
So, two by two, in line with Nature's plan,
You filled the Ark, and thus I came to see
How people tend to follow, hand in hand,
The way it used to be for you and me—
A pair of lovers strolling in the park,
A couple dreaming by a fireside,
Two others blowing bubbles, for a lark,
Or laughing at old movies, side by side.
Now you are gone, and I am left as one
Until we join as two in Kingdom come.

"Two by Two" was Bob's final portrait in verse to his most beloved teacher—his wife. Ever since Bob had met Shirley, he had admired how she loved animals. When she was young, Shirley had seven dogs, even though her mother was allergic to animals, and she devotedly took care of them, even nursing back to health a black and white spaniel, who had been impaled by a tree branch during a quail-hunting trip with Shirley's dad. Shirley loved to visit the St. Louis Zoo while growing up, and after she met Bob, she hardly missed an episode of Marlin Perkins's *Zoo Parade* from Lincoln Park Zoo in Chicago and, later, *Mutual of Omaha's Wild Kingdom.* She would become visibly upset when animals were mistreated in films. In the late 1970s Shirley began to collect miniature animals as a hobby. Carved exotic animals, painted ceramic pieces, and stuffed fabric ones marched toward Noah's Ark in her living room display, which she proudly showed to visitors.

Bob's poetic tribute to Shirley was one of many that touched on the personal aspects of his life. He, too, loved nature. He bonded with the pantheism of the early works of William Wordsworth, the belief that God is present in Nature and inseparable from it. This can be seen in such verse as "Experience with Nature," "The Seven and One Monarchs," "The Dove," and "When the Wakening Sun Is Golden." Bob also emulated Emerson in relating his poetry to his own life. Henry David Thoreau once wrote, "My life has been the poem I would have writ, / But I could not both live and utter it." Bob *did* both live and utter it.

On September 12, 2003, "Two By Two," a poem written with much tenderness and printed on the back page of a program for Shirley's memorial service in the Robert F. Panara

Theatre at NTID, was a poem that touched the hearts of everyone. At the memorial service, John talked about his mother's character and shared many loving memories. Hundreds of former students, colleagues, and friends came from around the country to comfort Bob, who told stories about his life with Shirley. As he stood at the podium, glanced back at the picture of Shirley projected onto a large screen in the Panara Theatre, he smiled softly as he spoke about the "keys to a successful marriage," giving us all one more lesson as a great teacher. "We learned to give and take. We learned to respect each other, and we learned the importance of having a good sense of humor. That carried us 56 years."

Over the next month, Bob spent some private moments with his granddaughter Erin, who adored her grandparents. Shirley was extremely proud of the lyrics Erin had written for some songs produced on a CD in collaboration with friends. Erin had written the lyrics for all ten songs, and the CD was dedicated to her grandmother. Bob also established the Shirley M. Panara Endowed Fund at NTID to honor the enthusiastic participation and love for the theater that Shirley shared from its inception as the Drama Club in 1970. To honor Shirley's vocation as a librarian, the endowment's focus will be to support activities that preserve past and future NTID Theatre performances through the archiving of materials connected with the theater, such as playbills, photographs, scripts, videotapes, books, films, and artworks.

Several months passed before Bob and I began again our work together. He had found some notes Shirley planned to give me for the biography. It was doubly hard to read them with her gone. I wondered if his heart and soul could handle the grief. One evening, I came upon a passage in the biography Bob had given me of my baseball hero Roberto Clemente. It was two years after Clemente's death when his wife Vera said about the loss of her husband: "It's something *always* inside you."[13]

On February 4, 2004, I received more sad news from Bob. He had lost King Pup. His dog had battled cancer and could not walk anymore. Heartbroken, Bob knew that King Pup had to be put to sleep. "And now I am all alone in this house," Bob wrote to me. "A house that was once so full of joy and alive with togetherness is now a ghostly reminder of the past."

I took him out to dinner that night at his favorite restaurant. We talked into the late hours, and he showed me a poem he had written in 1976, nearly thirty years earlier, titled "Man's Best Friend."

Afterword

In 2005 Bob told me a fish story about how in 1953 he had landed a ninety-six-pound tuna while on a boat with his dad in Cape Cod Bay. Knowing that I would pressure him to provide some evidence, he accompanied it with a newspaper clipping that included a photograph of himself, his dad, a friend, and the fish. "I felt like Santiago," Bob signed to me, "the titular old man of Ernest Hemingway's novel *The Old Man and the Sea*. Reminiscing about how both of his hands had cramped for a good half hour after the long battle with the hefty fish (see p. 98), Bob, with his amazing memory for lines from poems and novels, echoed Santiago's words, "I think the great DiMaggio would be proud of me today!"[1]

I had never read *The Old Man and the Sea*. During my undergraduate and graduate years studying physics and electrical engineering, I had had little time to read many of the literary classics. Over the years since I completed my degrees, however, my wife, Bonnie, had recommended many books to help me catch up. I began with F. Scott Fitzgerald's *The Great Gatsby* and followed that with several of E. M. Forster's novels, the poetry of Emily Dickinson, and many other works. But

Hemingway's *The Old Man and the Sea* had escaped me, and on this evening I was enjoying it as I sought the DiMaggio quote. After finally locating the quote and marking down the page number, I turned to Bonnie and discussed the book for a while. We had visited Hemingway's home in Key West, and we talked briefly about the visit that night. Afterwards, I placed the book on my bed stand and drifted asleep.

I can't explain the eerie event that occurred the next morning. Unable to sleep during the early morning hours, I sat up and turned on the television. After rubbing my eyes for a minute until I could focus in the dark room, I realized that the cable TV channel I had left on the night before was now showing an old black and white film with Spencer Tracy. The first captions I read on the screen were the exact words of the quote I had been looking for the night before in the book on my bed stand! "I think the great DiMaggio would be proud of me today!"[2]

My mind was not playing tricks on me. This was purely a coincidence, and a strange one at that. Maybe this story demonstrates that I could follow all of the advice I discussed in the Foreword of this book about writing a biography of a living person—except one— "staying free of the shadow cast by a respected subject." It is no surprise that the affinity we developed as biographer and subject led Bob and me to become best friends.

Since Shirley's death, I have assumed the daunting responsibility of "playing the spouse" on our baseball outings to Frontier Field, making sure Bob had his keys and a jacket in case the evening turned cool and helping him resist the urge to increase his cholesterol. For years, Bob's wife had frequently cautioned me as we left the house not to allow Bob to have too many Italian sausage sandwiches. We'd debate Shirley's wisdom in front of the concession stand for ten minutes and then make a decision. We batted about .500 on that issue.

Bob's section at Frontier Stadium is a happy family of season ticket holders who greet him like a brother or father. They have grown used to seeing Bob signing "Take Me Out to the Ballgame" during the seventh-inning stretch. Most of the "family" members in Bob's section do not know sign language, but they communicate with him well. They know that this man is special. Just as Jackie Robinson taught people, through baseball, about race, Bob has taught many of the hearing people in his section of the stadium about the art of being "Deaf." He is an equal to them in every important regard.

The story of Bob Panara's experiences as a deaf man who became a master teacher offers insight into the many debates going on in his field, Deaf education. Bob spent endless hours searching for a way to integrate the many aspects of his life into a whole through meaningful teaching. As William Shakespeare wrote in *As You Like It,* "One man in his time plays many parts." Bob strove to make advances in classes in which deaf students were fully integrated by virtue of his teaching. Poetry and literature were components he sought to incorporate into the architecture of his teaching. Bob saw NTID as a place to experiment with innovative approaches to learning that, as he later stated, "I believe, will be of value to hearing students and to the entire field of education of the deaf."[3] As Bob's colleague Bruce Halverson pointed out, it is interesting that "the first teacher hired at NTID wasn't a professor who specialized in a technical area but an English professor, Bob Panara, who taught dramatic literature and theatre."[4] Bob spent his hours hoping to reconcile the many dichotomies in the field of Deaf education. These included the debate about whether to sign or to speak, the relevance of the humanities in technical education, and the questions of how to address the needs and interests of deaf and hearing students in integrated classes and how to succeed personally and professionally in both the Deaf community and in mainstream society. But it was the "heart and soul" in his teaching, not the windmills he fought, that have touched the lives of generations of students.

Bob's life might best be summarized with a quotation from a letter written to him by his former student Taras Denis when Bob received an honorary doctorate from Gallaudet University in 1986. Denis wrote, "Yes, the ripples you made forty years ago are now waves crashing on distant shores."[5] Those "ripples" are what Bob Panara's life is all about today. A great teacher, he is surrounded by fans, young and old, who have found him an inspiring guide to life.

Now as I sit with Bob in his box seats at Frontier Stadium located between third base and home just a few rows up from the field, I look down to the dugout and think of that magical moment when Bob shook hands with Babe Ruth. It was the stuff of a young boy's dreams. And, in his own field, Bob became a major league teacher with a grand slam career.[6]

Notes

FOREWORD

1. "Two Staffers Look Back: Reflections of Ten Years," *NTID Focus* (Winter/Spring 1979): 20.

2. Ibid.

3. Panara, "The Significance of the Reading Problem." *Buff and Blue* 53 (1944): 17–25.

4. John Simon, "On the Kazan Front," *New York Times,* Nov. 27, 2005.

5. Sanjay Suri, "A Word for V S Naipaul," *Pakistan Daily Times,* Sept. 20, 2002.

6. Jay Parini, "Distinct Approaches to Biography, With Bellow and Updike as the Subjects," *Chronicle of Higher Education,* Nov. 30, 2000: B14.

MAGIC

1. Panara to Lang, Apr. 26, 2003.

2. Ibid.

3. Ibid.

THE SILENT HOURS STEAL ON

1. Panara to Lang, Apr. 23, 2003.
2. Ibid.
3. Panara to Lang, May 24, 2003.
4. Robert F. Panara, *On His Deafness and Other Melodies Unheard* (Rochester, N.Y.: Deaf Life Press, 1997), 12.
5. Panara to Lang, May 24, 2003.
6. Panara to Lang, May 21, 2003.

FINDING A DEAF IDENTITY

1. Robert F. Panara, student essay, "How I Look at Things in General." Gallaudet College, 1940.
2. Robert F. Panara, "Beginnings," *Missouri Record* 100, no. 1 (Oct. 1977): 2.
3. Ibid.
4. Panara, "Beginnings," 2.
5. Ibid.
6. Ibid.
7. Robert F. Panara, "What Are You Going to Be After Graduation?" *Maryland Bulletin* 84, no. 2 (Nov. 1963): 28.
8. Panara to Lang, Mar. 2, 2004.
9. "Robert F. Panara: As If for the First Time, an Interview," in *The Tactile Mind, Freedom*, ed. John Lee Clark (Minneapolis: Tactile Mind Press, 2001), 31.

ON THE CARPET

1. Robert F. Panara, student essay, Gallaudet College, Fall 1945.

2. Robert F. Panara to Eric Malzkuhn, personal communication, Mar. 21, 2001.

3. Panara to Lang, Apr. 23, 2003.

4. Panara to Lang, July 10, 2004.

5. Panara, student essay, Gallaudet College, Fall 1945.

6. Robert F. Panara to Ed Carney, personal communication, Sept. 6, 1994. Years later, Bob's "remembrance of our youthful ways" was summarized in a poem called "To You, My College Chums," which was warmly received by his former classmates.

7. Panara to Lang, Mar. 6, 2004.

8. Ibid.

9. Panara, student essay, Gallaudet College, Fall 1945.

10. Panara, student essay.

11. Panara to Lang, July 9, 2004.

THE LAUREATE OF KENDALL GREEN

1. Panara to Lang, July 9, 2004.

2. Panara to Lang, Aug. 5, 2004.

3. Panara to Lang, Mar. 4, 2004.

4. "Thermopylae" is printed in its entirety in Bob's book *On His Deafness and Other Melodies Unheard* (Rochester, N.Y.: Deaf Life Press, 1997.

THE SIGNIFICANCE
OF READING

1. Panara, student essay, Gallaudet College, Fall 1945.

2. Panara to Lang, Dec. 2, 2003.

3. "Panara: As If for the First Time," 32.

4. Panara, "The Significance of the Reading Problem," 17–25.

5. Ibid.

6. Panara, "Reading Problem."

7. Ibid.

8. Panara, "Reading Problem," 7.

9. Ibid.

10. Ibid.

11. Ibid.

SCULPTURES IN THE AIR

1. Panara to Lang, July 11, 2006.

2. http://www.deafdc.com/blog/oscar-ocuto/2006-03-09/robert-f-panaraa-master-amongst-men/ (Posted Mar. 9, 2006, by Oscar Ocuto, DeafDC.com).

IN FRONT OF THE CLASSROOM

1. Bernard Bragg, *Lessons in Laughter: The Autobiography of a Deaf Actor* (Washington, D.C.: Gallaudet University Press, 1989), 21.

2. Ibid., 23.

3. Ibid., 67.

4. Bragg, *Lessons,* 22.

5. Ibid., 21.

6. Ibid., 22.

7. Ibid., 22.

8. Bernard Bragg, interview with author, May 19, 2006.

9. Panara to Lang, Nov. 2, 2003.

ON HIS DEAFNESS

1. Elizabeth Drew, *Discovering Poetry* (New York: W. W. Norton, 1933).

2. Robert F. Panara, "On His Deafness," *American Annals of the Deaf,* 91, no. 2 (1946). Bob later modified the poem slightly.

3. Marilyn Darch, "Poetry in Motion," *Buffalo Courier Express,* Nov. 15, 1981.

4. Ibid.

5. H. G. Lang and B. Meath-Lang, "Joachim Du Bellay," in *Deaf Persons in the Arts and Sciences: A Biographical Dictionary* (Westport, Conn.: Greenwood Press, 1995), 98–101.

6. Lou Fant, *Say It with Hands* (Silver Spring, Md.: National Association of the Deaf, 1964).

GO WITH YOUR HEART

1. "Sunday Today: Robert Panara," NBC Channel 13 News, Mar. 14, 1988, Video 5925, National Technical Institute for the Deaf, Rochester Institute of Technology, Rochester, N.Y.

2. Shirley Panara, Reminiscences. Courtesy of Robert F. Panara.

3. Greg Livadas, "Deaf Librarian Also Was a Sports Enthusiast," *Rochester Democrat and Chronicle*, July 18, 2003, 4B.

4. Shirley Panara, Reminiscences. Robert F. Panara to Harry G. Lang, Aug. 9, 2003.

5. Ibid.

6. Panara to Lang, Dec. 30, 2003.

7. Leonard M. Elstad to Robert F. Panara, personal communication, Nov. 12, 1948.

8. Panara to Lang, Sept. 20, 2005.

RETURN TO KENDALL GREEN

1. "Gallaudet's Three New Faculty Members," *Buff and Blue*, Oct. 19, 1949, 1.

2. Shirley Panara, Reminiscences. Robert F. Panara to Harry G. Lang, Aug. 9, 2003.

3. Percival Hall to Robert F. Panara, personal communication, Dec. 14, 1952.

4. Panara to Lang, Mar. 6, 2004.

5. Robert F. Panara, "Turnabout," *College English* 13, no. 6 (Mar. 1952): 330.

6. Helen Powers, *Signs of Silence: Bernard Bragg and the National Theatre of the Deaf* (New York: Dodd, Mead & Company, 1972), 72.

7. Benjamin M. Schowe to Ray Stallo, July 24, 1953 (http://dspace.wrlc.org/doc/handle/2041/1134).

8. T. L. Anderson, "What of the Sign Language?" *American Annals of the Deaf* 83 (1938): 122.

9. Ibid., 127.

10. Robert F. Panara to Jane Maher, personal communication, Aug. 13, 1991.

11. Jane Maher, *Seeing Language in Sign: The Work of William C. Stokoe* (Washington, D.C.: Gallaudet University Press, 1996), 45.

12. Robert F. Panara, Humanities 202 Assignment, Gallaudet College, Feb. 1955.

13. "'The Silent Muse Anthology' by Robert F. Panara '45," *Gallaudet Alumni Bulletin* (Spring 1960): 3, 4, 9.

14. Ibid.

15. Eve Edstrom, "Lip Readers by Telescope Recorded Chats by Queen at Terp Grid Game," *Washington Post,* Nov. 16, 1957.

16. "How the Queen Saw an Odd New Game—And What She Said," *Life,* Oct. 28, 1957, 30.

17. Ibid.

18. Panara to Lang, Sept. 3, 2003.

19. "Prof. Panara, Alton Silvers Play Major Role in *Life*'s 'Operation Lipread,'" *Buff and Blue,* Nov. 1957, p. 6.

20. Ibid.

21. *Rochester Democrat and Chronicle,* Mar. 27, 1988.

FIAT LUX!

1. Jim Mathis, "Only College for Deaf Offers Ultimate in Educational Fields," *Houston Post,* May 11, 1959.

2. Ibid.

3. Jack Gannon to Harry G. Lang, personal communication, June 15, 2006.

4. Ibid.

5. Patrick Graybill to Harry G. Lang, personal communication, June 6, 2006.

6. Ibid.

7. Frances Parsons to Harry G. Lang, personal communication, May 14, 2006.

8. "An Interview with Ray," Educational Support Service Personnel *Network News* 18, no. 2 (Nov.–Dec. 2003).

9. *Tower Clock* 1961, 3.

10. "D.C. Expert Stresses Abilities of the Deaf," (Washington, D.C.) *Catholic Standard*, July 13, 1962, 16.

11. "The Silent Muse," *British Deaf News* 3 (1961): 103–4.

12. Robert F. Panara (1962). "Direct English Learning in the Upper School," Proceedings of the Convention of American Instructors of the Deaf, June 1961, 32.

13. Ibid., p. 36.

14. Panara to Lang, Aug. 1, 2004.

15. Ibid.

16. Ibid.

17. Ibid.

18. Bernard Bragg to Robert F. Panara, personal communication, 1962.

19. John Panara to Harry Lang, personal communication, June 4, 2004.

20. Margery Hall to Robert F. Panara, personal communication, Aug. 23, 1963.

MENDING WALL

1. John Gardner to Robert F. Panara, personal communication, Nov. 2, 1965.

2. Ibid.

3. Harry G. Lang and Karen N. Conner, *From Dream to Reality: The National Technical Institute for the Deaf, a College of the Rochester Institute of Technology* (Rochester, N.Y.: Rochester Institute of Technology, 2001).

4. Robert F. Panara to Ralph L. Hoag, personal communication, Nov. 5, 1987.

5. Lang and Conner, *From Dream to Reality*, 38.

6. Lang and Conner, *From Dream to Reality*, 6.

7. Greg Livadas, "A Lifetime as Mentor, Scholar and Teacher," *Rochester Democrat and Chronicle*, Feb. 12, 1995, 9A.

8. Panara to Lang, personal communication, July 19, 2004.

FIELD OF DREAMS

1. Lang and Conner, *From Dream to Reality*, 38.

2. Panara to Lang, Jan. 25, 2007.

3. Jack Gould, "TV: Theater of the Deaf on Channel 4," *New York Times*, April 3, 1967. Reprinted in the National Theatre of the Deaf program for the Rochester performance.

4. Lang and Conner, *From Dream to Reality*, 38.

5. Robert F. Panara, unpublished anecdote, n.d.

6. Robert F. Panara, "Cultural Arts Among Deaf People," *Gallaudet Today* 13 (1983): 13.

7. Ibid.

8. William C. Stokoe, Dorothy Casterline, and Carl Croneberg, *A Dictionary of American Sign Language on Linguistic Principles* (Washington, D.C.: Gallaudet College Press, 1965).

9. Robert F. Panara to Jane Maher, personal communication, Aug. 13, 1991.

10. Robert F. Panara, "The Simultaneous Method as Multi-Media," in *Accent on Unity: Horizons on Deafness,* ed. Harriet Green Kopp (Washington, D.C.: Council of Organizations Serving the Deaf, 1968,) 38–40.

11. Ibid., 40.

12. Robert Panara, "Poetry as a Language Learning Tool for Deaf Persons," paper presented at the International Research Seminar on the Vocational Rehabilitation of Deaf Persons, p. 150.

13. Lynne Bohlman, "Robert Panara, A Major League Teacher," *NTID Focus* (Winter–Spring 1993): 15.

14. Robert F. Panara, "The Silent Language and the National Theatre of the Deaf—An Introduction," paper presented at the National Conference on Visual Literacy, Rochester, N.Y., 1969.

15. "Two Staffers Look Back: Reflections of Ten Years," *NTID Focus* (Winter/Spring 1979): 20.

16. John Machacek, "Body Movement for Dramatic Expression," *Rochester Times Union,* Dec. 12, 1970, 4C.

17. Ibid.

18. Ibid.

19. Ibid.

NOTHING GREAT—
WITHOUT ENTHUSIASM

1. James H. Higgs III, "It's a Deaf, Deaf, Deaf, Deaf World!" *Deaf American* 27 (1974): 3–4.

2. Ibid.

3. Ibid.

4. Chuck Jones to Harry G. Lang, personal communication, Apr. 15, 2006.

5. Robert F. Panara, "The Deaf Writer in America From Colonial Times to 1970," *American Annals of the Deaf* (Sept. 1970): 679.

6. Robert F. Panara, "Deaf Characters in Fiction and Drama," *Deaf American* (May 1972): 6.

7. Nancy Anderson, "Robert Panara Characterizes NTID Dream," *NTID Focus* (June 1971): 9.

8. Ibid.

9. Robert F. Panara, "Dr. Powrie V. Doctor (Pro Memoria)," *Gallaudet Today* 2, no. 1 (Fall 1971): 23.

10. Newton Dillaway, ed., *The Gospel of Emerson* (Boston: Beacon Press, 1949), 10.

11. Harley Parker, "Sound of Vision Conference," Rochester Institute of Technology, Unpublished transcripts, October 25, 1973: 24

12. Ibid., 25.

13. Lang and Conner, *From Dream to Reality.*

14. Robert F. Panara, NTID dedication speech, Oct. 5, 1974.

15. Panara to Lang, July 9, 2006.

16. "Focus on People," *NTID Focus* (Oct. 1969): 3.

17. "Experimental Educational Theatre," *NTID Focus* (Mar.–Apr. 1974): 7.

18. "Panara: As If for the First Time," 34.

19. Panara to Lang, Feb. 28, 2005.

20. John Panara to Lang, Nov. 2004.

21. Robert F. Panara, "Beginnings," commencement address given to the Kendall Demonstration Elementary School, 1975.

22. Later Bob closely followed the careers of deaf football players Bonnie Sloan of the NFL's St. Louis Cardinals and Kenny Walker of the Denver Broncos, and, baseball player Curtis Pride.

23. Panara, "Cultural Arts among Deaf People," 14.

24. "Panara: As If for the First Time."

25. Kathleen Sullivan, "Sign Language: Ticket to Success for RIT Grad." *NTID Focus* (Winter 1981): 25.

26. Ibid.

BEING AND READING

1. Sullivan, "Ticket to Success."

2. Robert F. Panara, "On Teaching Poetry to the Deaf (Or: Let the Student Be the Poem!)," *American Annals of the Deaf* 124, no. 7: 825.

3. Ibid. 827–28.

4. *NTID Focus* (Winter–Spring 1979): 20.

5. Robert F. Panara, "A Deaf Visiting Professor at CSUN," NTID internal report, Fall, 1976: 2.

6. Panara, *On His Deafness,* 101.

7. "Expanding Expressive Language Through Poetry," The Video Difference, Inc., 1989.

8. Karen Beiter to Harry G. Lang, personal communication, Apr. 6, 2006.

9. Ibid.

10. Ibid.

11. Ibid.

12. Ibid.

13. Panara to Lang, Feb. 2, 2007.

14. Bruce A. White, TEDSL Interview with Robert Panara. *Teaching English to Deaf and Second-Language Students* 2, no. 3 (Fall 1984): 13.

15. "Panara: As If For the First Time," 29–39.

16. Willy Conley to Harry G. Lang, personal communication, July 5, 2006.

17. Gerry Buckley to Harry G. Lang, personal communication, Mar. 24, 2006.

18. Alex Haley, "Thank You," in *College Writing Skills with Readings,* 5th ed., ed. John Langan (Boston: McGraw-Hill, 2001), 591.

19. Conley to Lang, July 5, 2006.

20. Jackie Schertz to Harry G. Lang, personal communication, Sept. 18, 2004.

21. Ann Kanter, "Campus Workshop Heralds Era of Signed Poetry: Allen Ginsberg," *NTID Focus* (Spring/Summer 1984): 22–25.

22. Ibid., 23.

23. Panara to Lang, July 14, 2004.

24. Kanter, "Campus Workshop," 25.

25. Interview with Jim Cohn by Maura Gage, Dec. 27–28, 2000. http://www.poetspath.com/jimcohnpoems/JCinterview.html.

26. Ibid.

DEFINING MOMENTS

1. Kathleen S. Smith, "NTID's Performing Arts Department Celebrates 20 Years of Entertainment," *NTID Focus* (Fall 1995): 17.

2. Jan Afzelius to Robert F. Panara, personal communication, July 7, 1988.

3. Gerald DeCoursey to Robert F. Panara, personal communication, Nov. 5, 1982.

4. Robert F. Panara to Rex Lowman, Dec. 12, 1983.

5. Lynne Bohlman, "Robert Panara: A Major League Teacher," *NTID Focus* (Winter/Spring 1993): 15.

6. Paul A. Miller to Robert F. Panara, personal communication, no date.

7. "Institute Announces Panara Scholarship Fund," *NTID Focus* (Fall 1987): 32.

8. Chuck Baird, handwritten notes dated Oct. 6, 1987.

9. Panara to Lang, Nov. 20, 2004.

10. Ibid.

MAKING A PITCH

1. Nicholas Dawidoff, ed., *Baseball: A Literary Anthology.* New York: Library of America, 2002.

2. Robert F. Panara to Eleanor and John Lynch, Nov. 5, 1990.

3. Harold Bloom, *Genius: A Mosaic of One Hundred Exemplary Creative Minds* (New York: Warner Books, 2002), 342.

4. Robert F. Panara to Darryl Brock, personal communication, Mar. 26, 1999.

5. Robert F. Panara, "Baseball Wouldn't be the Same without 'Dummy Hoy,'" *Rochester Democrat and Chronicle,* Sept. 9, 1990, 15A.

6. Robert F. Panara to Eric Malzkuhn, personal communication, Sept. 22, 1990.

7. Robert F. Panara, "'Dummy Hoy' Belongs in Cooperstown," *Silent News* (Oct. 1990): 36.

8. Robert F. Panara to Thomas C. Eakin, personal communication, Aug. 25, 1992.

9. Ibid.

10. Robert F. Panara to Eleanor and John Lynch, personal communication, June 26, 1991.

11. Robert F. Panara to Bert Lependorff, personal communication, Aug. 29, 1991.

12. Thomas C. Eakin to Veterans Committee, National Baseball Hall of Fame, Feb. 27, 1996.

13. Robert F. Panara to Scott Pitoniak, *Rochester Democrat and Chronicle,* Mar. 24, 1996.

14. Scott Pitoniak, "He Wants Hero in the Hall," *Rochester Times-Union,* Mar. 5, 1997, 1A, 7A.

15. Scott Pitoniak to Robert F. Panara, personal communication, Mar. 7, 1998.

16. Matt Leingang, "Going to Bat for a Deaf Hero," *Rochester Democrat and Chronicle,* Feb. 20, 2000, 8A.

17. Ibid.

18. Ibid.

19. Stephen Jay Gould, *Triumph and Tragedy in Mudville: A Lifelong Passion for Baseball* (New York: W. W. Norton, 2003), 129.

RUSTLE OF A STAR

1. Robert F. Panara to R. L. Hoag, Nov. 5, 1987.

2. "Expanding Expressive Language Through Poetry."

3. Erin Panara to Harry G. Lang, personal communication, Sept. 12, 2005.

4. Robert F. Panara to Rex Lowman, personal communication, Apr. 26, 1985.

5. Robert F. Panara to Eleanor and John Lynch, personal communication, Oct. 28, 1996.

6. I. King Jordan to Robert F. Panara, personal communication, Oct. 23, 1998.

7. Panara to Lang, Mar. 11, 2006.

8. Panara, "Cultural Arts Among Deaf People," 13.

9. Robert F. Panara to George Propp, personal communication, Dec. 18, 1995.

10. Conley to Lang, July 5, 2006.

11. "Panara: As If For the First Time," 37.

12. Jeanne Behm to Harry G. Lang, personal communication, July 12, 2006.

13. Noreen Collins to Robert F. Panara, personal communicaiton, Dec. 23, 1987.

14. Panara to Malzkuhn, May 7, 2001.

HEART AND SOUL

1. White, "TEDSL Interview with Robert Panara," 14.

2. Alex Haley, "Thank You," 591.

3. Alan Gifford to Harry G. Lang, personal communication, July 12, 2006.

4. John Panara to Harry G. Lang, personal communication, June 4, 2004.

5. Robert F. Panara to Lang, Aug. 1, 2005.

6. Greg Livadas, "A Lifetime as Mentor, Scholar and Teacher," *Rochester Democrat and Chronicle,* Feb. 12, 1995, 9A.

7. Robert F. Panara, Humanities 202 Assignment, Gallaudet College, Feb. 1955.

8. Robert F. Panara, "A Note on Santayana's Sense of Beauty," *Buff and Blue Literary Magazine* (Washington, D.C.: Gallaudet College, 1956): 11.

9. Panara to Lang, July 10, 2003.

10. Ibid.

11. Friedrich Halm, *Der Sohn der Wildniss,* Act II.

12. Panara to Lang, July 3, 2005.

13. Jim O'Brien, *Remember Roberto* (Pittsburgh: Geyer Printing Company, 1994), 38.

AFTERWORD

1. Ernest Hemingway, *The Old Man and the Sea* (New York: Charles Scribner's Sons, 1952), 96.

2. Ibid.

3. "Focus on People," *NTID Focus* (October 1969): 3.

4. Bruce R. Halverson, "Deaf and Hearing Together," in *Perspectives: A Handbook in drama and theatre, by, with, and for handicapped individuals,* ed. Ann Shaw, Wendy Perks, and C. J. Stevens (Washington, D.C.: American Theatre Association, 1981), 3–16.

5. Taras B. Denis to Robert F. Panara, personal communication, June 14, 1985.

6. Lynne Bohlman, "Robert Panara: A Major League Teacher," *NTID Focus* (Winter/Spring 1993): 15.

References

Higgs, James H., III. "It's a Deaf, Deaf, Deaf, Deaf World!" *Deaf American* 27 (1950): 3–4.

Kanter, Ann. "Campus Workshop Heralds Era of Signed Poetry: Allen Ginsberg." *NTID Focus* (Spring/Summer 1984): 22–25.

Lang, Harry G., and Karen N. Conner. *From Dream to Reality: The National Technical Institute for the Deaf, A College of Rochester Institute of Technology.* Rochester, N.Y.: Rochester Institute of Technology, 2001.

Lang, Harry G., and Bonnie Meath-Lang. "Robert F. Panara, Educator." In *Deaf Persons in the Arts and Sciences: A Biographical Dictionary* (Westport, Conn.: Greenwood Press, 1995), 287–90.

Levitan, Linda, and Matthew S. Moore. "A tribute to Bob Panara." *Deaf Life* 1, no. 3 (1988), 14–21.

Machacek, John. "Body Movement for Dramatic Expression." Rochester, New York *Times Union*, December 12, 1970, 4C.

Maher, Jane. *Seeing Language in Sign: The Work of William C. Stokoe.* Washington, D.C.: Gallaudet University Press, 1996.

Moore, Matthew S., and Robert F. Panara. *Great Deaf Americans.* 2nd ed. Rochester, N.Y.: Deaf Life Press, 1996.

Panara, Robert F. "Beginnings." *Missouri Record* 100, no. 1 (Oct. 1977): 2, 20–22.

———. "Bernard Bragg: Master of Mime." *Gallaudet Alumni Bulletin* (Winter 1962): 3–6.

———. "The Big Four at Fanwood." *Volta Review* 50, no. 1 (1948): 7–8, 38, 40.

———. "Creative Approaches to Teaching/Interpreting Poetry to Deaf Students." First National Conference on the Visual and Performing Arts in the Education of Deaf Students. Phoenix, Ariz., Oct. 17, 1986.

———. "Cultural and Professional Values in the Field of English." *Gallaudet Alumini Bulletin* 3, no. 5 (1952): 10–11.

———. "Cultural Arts Among Deaf People." *Gallaudet Today* 13 (1983): 12–16.

———. "Deaf Characters in Fiction and Drama." *Deaf American* (May 1972): 3–8.

———. "Deaf Studies in the English curriculum." Proceedings of the Convention of American Instructors of the Deaf, 26, no. 5 (1974): 15.

———. "The deaf writer in America: 1900–1954." *The Silent Worker* (Oct. 1954): 3–5.

———. "The Deaf Writer in America from Colonial Times to 1970: Part 1." *American Annals of the Deaf* (Sept. 1970): 509–13.

———. "The Deaf Writer in America from Colonial Times to 1970: Part 2." *American Annals of the Deaf* (Nov. 1970): 673–79.

———. "Direct English Learning in the Upper School." Proceedings of the Convention of American Instructors of the Deaf, June 1961, 32–39.

———. "'Dummy Hoy' Belongs in Cooperstown." *Silent News* (Oct. 1990), 36.

———. "'Dummy' Hoy Enters Ohio Baseball Hall of Fame." *Deaf Life* 5, no. 4 (October 1992): 10–12.

———. "The Education of the Deaf." In *The New Catholic Encylopedia.* New York: McGraw-Hill, 1964, 681–82.

———. "Literary Analysis: A Uniform Approach to Interpreting Literature." Proceedings of the Convention of American Instructors of the Deaf, June 1965.

———. "My Greatest Thrill in Sports." In *Our Heritage: Gallaudet College Centennial.* Washington, D.C.: Gallaudet College, 1964.

———. "A Note on Santayana's Sense of Beauty." *The Buff and Blue Literary Magazine* (1956): 9–11.

———. "Oedipus Without Complexes." *Buff and Blue Literary Magazine* (Washington, D.C.: Gallaudet College, 1957).

———. "On Teaching Poetry to the Deaf (Or: Let the Student Be the Poem!)." *American Annals of the Deaf* 124, no. 7 (1979): 825–28.

———. "Poetry and the Deaf." *American Annals of the Deaf* 90, no. 4 (1945): 340–44.

———. "Poetry as a Language Learning Tool for Deaf Persons." Proceedings of the International Research Seminar on Education and Rehabilitation of the Deaf. Washington, D.C.: Social and Rehabilitation Service, June 1968, 146–51.

———. "The problem of identity in the works of Ralph Waldo Emerson." Submitted in partial fulfillment of the requirements for the degree of master of arts at New York University, 1948.

———. *On His Deafness and Other Melodies Unheard.* Rochester, N.Y.: Deaf Life Press, 1997.

———. "Secondary Language Preparation and NTID." Proceedings of the 44th Convention of American Instructors of the Deaf, Washington, D.C.: CAID, June 1969, 306–12.

———. "The significance of the reading problem." *Buff and Blue* 53 (1944): 17–25.

———. "The Silent Muse Anthology." *Gallaudet Alumni Bulletin* 5 (Spring 1960): 3–4, 9.

———. "The Simultaneous Method as Multi-Media." In *Access on Unity: Horizons on Deafness.* Washington, D.C.: Council of Organizations Serving the Deaf, 1968, 38–40.

———. "So Near, Yet So Far: Rallying for 'Dummy' Hoy in Cooperstown." *Deaf Life* (Sept. 1997): 11–23.

———. "Total Communication for the Deaf." *Rehabilitation Record* (Jan.–Feb. 1971): 20–21.

———. "What Are You Going To Be After Graduation?" *Maryland Bulletin* 84, no. 2 (Nov. 1963): 17–18, 27–28.

Panara, Robert F., Taras B. Denis, and John McFarlane, eds. *The Silent Muse* (Washington, D.C.: Gallaudet College Alumni Association, 1960).

Panara, Robert F., and John Panara. *Great Deaf Americans.* Silver Spring, Md.: T. J. Publishers, 1983.

Pearson, Lester B. "Panara appointed to NTID advisory board." *Gallaudet Record* 11, no. 5 (Jan. 1966): 4.

Pitoniak, Scott. "He Wants Hero in the Hall," *Rochester Times Union,* March 5, 1997, 1A & 3A.

"Poetry & Sign,"*Just Buffalo,* Final Report 1981, Special Constituencies Model Project sponsored by the New York State Council on the Arts and the National Endowment for the Arts. Buffalo, N.Y.: Just Buffalo, 1981.

Powers, Helen. *Signs of Silence: Bernard Bragg and the National Theatre of the Deaf.* New York: Dodd, Mead & Company, 1972.

Stokoe, William C., Dorothy Casterline, and Carl Croneberg. *A Dictionary of American Sign Language on Linguistic Principles.* Washington, D.C.: Gallaudet College Press, 1965.

Taub, Peter B. "Panara presents." *Mt. Airy World* 86, no. 3 (Feb.– Mar. 1972): 23, 28.

White, Bruce A. TEDSL Interview with Robert Panara. *Teaching English to Deaf and Second-Language Students* 2, no. 3 (Fall 1984): 12–19.

"Robert F. Panara: As If for the First Time, an Interview." In *The Tactile Mind, Freedom* (Minneapolis: Tactile Mind Press, 2001).

"Where do we go from here?: A scoop, a palpable scoop!" *The Reporter* [New York], Dec. 12, 1957, 4–5.

"Prof. Panara, Alton Silvers play major role in *Life*'s 'Operation Lipread,'" *Buff and Blue,* vol. 63, no.2, Nov. 1957: 1.